'Not Of 7

The story of
Norfolk's Monastic Houses
in the Middle Ages

by
Frank Meeres

2001

First published 2001 by Frank Meeres.

© Frank Meeres, 2001.

All rights reserved. No part of this publication may be produced, stored in a retrieval system, or transmitted in any form or by any means, electronic, mechanical, photocopying, recording, or otherwise, without the prior permission of the Copyright owner.

ISBN 0-9541153-0-9

Printed by Rigby Print, Norwich.

CONTENTS

List of illustrations	v
Introduction	1
The beginnings	3
The monks	8
The canons	17
The military orders	23
The nuns	27
Hermits and anchorites	35
The friars	37
The buildings	50
How they lived - daily life	74
How they lived - income and expenditure	93
The end	125
Further reading	137
Gazeteer of Norfolk religious houses	139
Index	146

ACKNOWLEDGEMENTS

This book could not have been written without the kind support of the Norfolk Record Office (County Archivist Dr John Alban): I am grateful for permission to reproduce documents in the care of the Record Office. I would also like to thank Helen Jones for her work in typing the manuscript of this book and Irene McLaughlin for designing the graph and charts.

ILLUSTRATIONS

ENDPAPERS:

FRONT: Richard Taylor's map of Norfolk monastic site (from Index Monasticus)

BACK: Plan of St Benet's abbey precinct, by Arthur Whittingham

COLOUR ILLUSTRATIONS (between pages 70 and 71) :

1	St Augustine writing on a scroll. From the pulpit in Burnham Norton parish church (NRO, MC 640/4/8)

2	Graph to show the dates of foundation of Norfolk religious houses

3	List of people and the mortuaries they gave in return for burial in the cemetery of Marham abbey (NRO, Hare 1)

4	Early printed service book from Langley abbey: unusually this is printed onto parchment rather than paper (NRO, NRS 19869)

5	The Monastic Day: Summer

6	The Monastic Day: Winter

7	Portrait of Robert Catton, the prior of Norwich Cathedral, surrounded by his monks and holding a charter, 1524 (NRO, NCR 9g)

8 & 9	Two scenes from the retable in Norwich Cathedral priory, probably a gift from Bishop Henry Despenser (NRO, DCN 125/3)

10	Bromholme: the gatehouse with a pilgrims' guest-house in the distance

11	Burnham Norton friary: the gate-house

12	The isolation of a Norfolk monastic house: Langley abbey

13	Drawing by John Adey Repton of Norwich Cathedral priory cloister (NRO, COL 8/11/2)

14   St Benedict (left), with another Benedictine saint. From the pulpit at Horsham St Faith parish church

15   Marham abbey rent roll (NRO, Hare 2213)

16   Castle Acre: the latrine block or reredorter

BLACK AND WHITE ILLUSTRATIONS:

1   Anthony Norris' drawing of St Benet's abbey. Although this looks like an accurate drawing, it is not: the church had a west tower as well as the central one and no aisles to the nave. (NRO, RYE 6)

2   Binham priory: the west front.

3   The Bucks' view of Wymondham abbey (NRO, MS 4579)

4   Interior of Norwich Cathedral priory, showing monks' stalls. (NRO, from MC 186/84)

5   Castle Acre: the west front (NRO, from MC 186/84)

6   Bromholme priory: the ivy has since been cleared from the ruins (NRO, MC 365/2)

7   Walsingham priory: the east end of the church (NRO, MC 530/2)

8   Creake abbey: the chancel, transepts and chapels, taken from the site of the nave

9   Weybourne priory

10   Beeston priory: the chancel

11   The church of the canons of the Holy Sepulchre at Thetford, the only surviving building in England of this order of canons.

12   Ingham church: the sacrist lived in the upper storey of the porch

13   Remains of the cloister on the north side of Ingham church

14	Modern house built into the remnants of Thetford nunnery
15	Marham abbey showing the line of the cloister roof with the rose windows above
16	Nuns or donors? Skeletons in stone coffins found at Thetford nunnery in 1908 (NRO, MC 365/153)
17	The Briton's Arms in Norwich: a medieval beguinage?
18	St Francis of Assisi displays his stigmata (left), the only surviving representation of St Francis on a Norfolk screen. The other figure is St Leonard, in the dress of a medieval monk. From the screen at Hempstead next Eccles parish church (NRO, PD 273/29)
19	Reconstruction drawing of Norwich Dominican friary by Benjamin Sewell.
20	Yarmouth Franciscan friary: the west walk of the cloister
21	Arch from Norwich Carmelite friary reused at Arminghall Old Hall: the arch is now in Norwich Magistrates' Court (NRO, from MC 186/84)
22	The tower of Lynn Franciscan friary
23	Brass to friar William Yarmouth, now at Halvergate parish church
24	Wendling abbey, marked to show typical features of a monastery. (Based on drawing in NRO, MS 4580)
25	Binham priory: Bucks' drawing, showing the west end window. (NRO, MS 4579)
26	Interior of Binham priory
27	Norwich Cathedral priory: tower and spire (NRO, ACCN Clark 18/10/91)
28	Ingham: the remains of the stone pulpitum, with monks' stalls beyond
29	Wymondham priory church: the part between the two towers has been maintained as the parish church of the town (NRO, MC 640/22/4/1)

30   Map of Blakeney in 1586, showing friary church and parish church (NRO, MC 106/28/1)

31   Aldeby church: as a monastic cell of the cathedral priory, this was a superior building for a village church, with north and south transepts (NRO, MS 4576)

32   Monastic plans (1) Thetford St Mary priory

33   Monastic plans (2) Norwich Dominican friary

34   Wymondham chapter house arch

35   Norwich Cathedral priory: the monk's dining room

36   Thetford St Mary: the monks' dining room

37   Norwich Cathedral priory: the guest quarters

38   Thetford St Mary: the prior's lodging

39   Beeston priory: the north transept, with the pond to the north of the church (NRO, MC 530/8)

40   Pentney: the gatehouse

41   Castle Acre gatehouse, before its restoration by English Heritage (NRO, MC 530/8)

42   Walsingham Franciscan friary (NRO, MS 4579)

43   A monk reading, a misericord in Norwich Cathedral priory (NRO, MC 186/82)

44   The central portion of the Thornham Parva retable, originally painted for Thetford Dominican priory

45   Walsingham Austin priory: the dining room

46   Thetford St Mary: infirmary cloister

viii

47 Westacre: All Saints parish church and the monastery gatehouse

48 Trowse parish church: the east window designed by the Norwich Cathedral priory mason

49 St Benet's abbey: the gatehouse drawn by John Kirkpatrick in the early 18th century, shortly before it was made into a windmill (NRO, RYE 17 vol. 6)

50 Thetford Warren Lodge photographed during the fire of 1 August 1935 (NRO, MC 365/150)

51 Walsingham Austin priory seal (from Victoria County History available on NRO searchroom shelves)

52 A pilgrim emerges from a shell (a common badge of pilgrimage). From a Norwich Cathedral priory misericord (NRO, MC 186/82)

53 Brass to Geoffrey Langley, prior of Horsham St Faith. This drawing was made while the brass was at Norwich St Lawrence church: the lower half is now in Horsham St Faith parish church (NRO, MC 1741/31)

54 Ingham church, showing the monks' stalls and the monuments (NRO, RYE 139)

55 Schoolteacher spanking a pupil. From a Norwich Cathedral priory misericord (NRO, MC 186/82)

56 The prior's hall, Great Yarmouth Benedictine priory: this photograph was taken in the 1860s, after the building had become a school (NRO, Y/TC 86/12/64)

57 Creake abbey in the mid-nineteenth century (NRO, MS 4576)

58 Dramatic view of St Benet's abbey gatehouse, showing the cap to the windmill, which has since disappeared. (NRO, from MC 186/84)

59 Remains of Hickling priory, now a farm (NRO, MC 530/2)

60 W.H. Cooke's drawing of Ingham priory, complete with ghost (NRO, MS 4311)

INTRODUCTION

When people think of medieval monasteries they think firstly of the great monastic ruins on the Yorkshire moors. Norfolk is probably not seen as an area particularly strong in monasticism, but in fact it had one of the largest numbers of monastic houses of any county in England. The concentration along the Nar valley is especially notable: the valley became known as 'Norfolk's Holy Land'. Although some of the religious houses have entirely disappeared, there are at least seven first-rate sites in the county that are open to visitors. Many of the sites with fewer remains are also worth a visit to appreciate something of the spirituality generated by the religious men and women who lived and worshipped there.

In the Middle Ages there were thought to be three paths that a man might follow to contribute to the community: he might work, he might fight or he might pray. (This threefold distinction was sometimes applied within the church itself - the parish priest laboured, the monks prayed, the military orders, discussed later, fought.) Belief in the existence of heaven and hell was universal, as was belief in the power of prayer and almsgiving to save one's soul. The assumption of one's deep and abiding guilt led to terror of the agonies of hell. This guilt could be alleviated by good deeds, especially by gifts to the church and to the poor. Herbert de Losinga, the founder of Norwich Cathedral priory, wrote that 'alms extinguish sin as water does fire'. Until the later twelfth century it was a simple matter of heaven or hell: the stark choice portrayed on the chancel arches of many parish churches where the horrors of hell were commonly depicted in lurid detail. From the 1160s the notion of purgatory developed, an intermediate state between heaven and hell where a soul might suffer for a time but eventually is released into heaven. This went alongside a belief that prayer could shorten the time in purgatory spent by oneself or one's forebears. This was where the monastery came in: monks and nuns, leading a pure life themselves in the service of God, were thought to be especially able to offer up prayers for the deceased and shorten the time of their sufferings. Thus the monastic house was seen as the fortress or powerhouse of prayer. As we shall see they had other functions too, especially in the field of charity and education. However the prime function was always prayer.

This book considers the origin of monasticism in Norfolk and its rapid growth under the Normans. It also considers special groups of religious people - monks, canons, the military orders, nuns and friars. It discusses how life was lived in a monastery, and what monastic churches and buildings looked like, with a special emphasis on surviving remains within Norfolk. It describes the process of dissolution of the monasteries in the 1530s and concludes with a gazetteer listing the monastic houses in Norfolk and assessing the state of the surviving buildings. The book has nearly eighty illustrations, each one of which relates directly to Norfolk, including several images taken from the rood screens for which the county is famous. Over half the illustrations are from material at the Norfolk Record Office, demonstrating the richness and variety of archive sources for the history of monasticism in the county.

THE BEGINNINGS

In all religions there have been men and women who have felt the call to dedicate their lives fully to their God, either on their own or in a community of like-minded people. Some of the earliest Christian communities of this kind developed out of groups of hermits in the deserts of Egypt. St Anthony is traditionally regarded as the father of Christian monasticism. He lived as a hermit in the desert from about 285 AD. By 305 AD his fame had spread and many followers had gathered around him which he formed into the first monastic community. Anthony lived to be 105 years old and we are told that when he died he still had all his teeth: the monastic life was clearly a healthy one!

Pachomius, another Egyptian recluse around whom followers gathered, took the next step. The monks in his monastery used to try and outdo each other in feats of fasting. It got to the stage where no one dared to eat anything for fear of being thought 'soft'. Pachomius' solution was a drastic one: he made all the monks wear large cowls or hoods. When the monks were at dinner their hoods covered their plates so that no one could see what each monk ate - or did not eat. By 315 AD he had developed a rule or set of instructions to avoid excessive self-sacrifice as well as laxity.

Basil, Bishop of Caesarea, developed another rule between 370 and 379. His rule stressed community life, liturgical prayer and manual labour. It allowed for the development of almsgiving, hospitals and guesthouses in which the monks worked. To this day, nearly all monks and nuns of the Greek church follow Basil's rule. The influence of 'our holy father Basil' was acknowledged by Benedict, the man whose rule was to form the basis of monastic life throughout Western Europe for the next thousand years. Benedict was born at Nursia in Italy in about 480 AD. He became a hermit at Subiaco where followers gathered around him, whom he had to organise. Later he moved to Monte Cassino where he wrote the final version of his rule. He was not a priest and never intended to found a religious order.

Like Pachomius before him, Benedict disapproved of the excessive self-discipline of some hermits. When a hermit near his monastery chained himself to a rock, Benedict rebuked him saying 'if you are God's servant, let the chain of Christ, not any iron chain hold you'. The Introduction to his rule explains its intention: *'We are about to institute a school for the service of God in which we hope nothing harsh nor burdensome will be ordained ... so that we never leaving His school, but persevering in the monastery until death in His teaching, may share, by our patience in the sufferings of Christ, and so merit to be partakers in His kingdom'.*

Benedict was clear that the monks should be busy all day - he wrote that 'idleness is the enemy of the soul'. His rule includes very detailed instructions for all the seven offices or services that were used each day. This OPUS DEI - the work of God - would have taken up about four hours of the day in winter months. The monks were also to do manual work - a letter by Pope Gregory describes an abbot mowing the hay alongside his monks. However, from almost the earliest days, there was already a division between monks who liked hard physical work and those who did not. Bede tells the story of an East Anglian monk called Owen. He was the master of the household to Etheldreda, the sister of Withburga of Dereham. He decided to become a monk and arrived at Lastingham monastery in his poorest clothes carrying an axe. He meant to 'work hard rather than pursue idleness in monastic life'. By the time of the Norman Conquest the only kind of work done by Benedictine monks involved copying of manuscripts.

Benedict also stressed the humility necessary for a monk. He must take a vow that he would stay at the monastery until death and he was to obey the abbot as if he were God. 'Abbot' comes from the Aramaic word 'abba' which means father and is used by Jesus in the New Testament. The abbot was the father of the community and to him was owed complete obedience. On entering the monastery a monk gave up his own clothes and took on the robes he was given. He was not allowed to own anything - *'none, without leave of the abbot, shall presume to give, or receive, or keep as his own, anything whatever: neither book nor tablets, nor pen: nothing at all'*. All monastic property was to be held in common.

Another important strand of the Benedictine Rule was the duty of hospitality. All guests must be welcomed and allowed to stay free of charge. As to the poor 'special attention should be shown because in them is Christ more truly welcomed'. Benedict also laid down rules as to diet - 'except the sick who are very weak, let all abstain from eating the flesh of four-footed animals'. This was not vegetarianism as we know it of course - fish could be eaten and also the flesh of birds. He was aware that the close-knit community of a monastery - like a marriage - could be made full of resentments by small details such as who was to do the washing-up. Under the rule, kitchen work was to be done by each monk in turn for a week: at the end of his weekly shift he must clean everything ready for the next monk.

The Beginnings

There is a direct link between St Benedict and English Christianity. As is well known, Pope Gregory the Great decided at the end of the sixth century to convert England to Christianity. He was a monk himself and a friend of Benedict. The men he sent were monks too and, if not formally dedicated to the rule of St Benedict, were clearly in sympathy with it - and of course had that vital monkish quality of unquestioning obedience.

The conversion of the Saxon kingdom of East Anglia began with King Sigebert, who had become a Christian while in exile in Gaul. The king welcomed Felix when he was sent by Archbishop Honorius to convert the East Anglians - Felix was a Frenchman. He was made bishop of 'Dommoc', traditionally thought to be Dunwich, but now thought likely to be at or just outside Felixstowe. There was another strand of monasticism, however, which also affected East Anglia. This spread from Celtic monastic communities in Ireland reaching Scotland and Northern England. It affected East Anglia too. Sigebert welcomed the Irish monks Fursey and his brother Foillan into his kingdom. He gave them a site to build a monastery at a place called Cnobheresburg. This was probably at Burgh Castle, as Sir Henry Spelman thought: he gave no archival evidence to support his opinions but archaeological work has revealed Middle Saxon occupation there. However it could have been in the Roman fort at Caister-on-Sea, near which a Middle Saxon cemetery has been found. There was disagreement between the two traditions about some aspects of Christianity, most famously about the date Easter was to be celebrated - eventually the matter was decided in favour of the Roman way of dating which still holds sway. After the mid-seventh century the Celtic monasteries in England gradually withered away as Benedictine monasticism triumphed. Its time in East Anglia was a short one - Fursey and Foillan retreated to France after Sigebert had been defeated in battle and killed by Penda, the pagan king of Mercia.

Other monasteries in Norfolk were founded in Saxon times but very little is known about them. Most were swept away in the Danish Conquest of East Anglia in the late ninth century. One example of a Saxon monastery in Norfolk was that at Dereham. This was supposedly founded by St Withburga, the youngest daughter of King Anna of East Anglia. (Her sister, Etheldreda, founded a community at Ely). Withburga died in about 743 and was buried in the churchyard. Fifty years later she was reburied in the church itself. In 974 Brithnoth, the abbot of Ely, and his monks stole the body from the church after getting the Dereham men drunk at a great feast. The townsmen chased after them to get the body back but they were thwarted when the abbot's men boarded boats they had previously hidden. The saint's name survives at East

Dereham in Withburga's well in the churchyard (tradition says this is the spot where she was originally buried). There are also paintings of her on six Norfolk church screens: she is often shown with a tame deer, which, according to legend, provided her with milk when she was thirsty. Scholars in recent years have suggested that the nunnery was actually at West Dereham rather than East Dereham: the story of the boats would certainly make more sense if this were the case as West Dereham is much closer to Ely and on the same river system. However the people of East Dereham are unlikely to give up their claim easily: the story of St. Withburga provides the theme for the town sign across the main road near the Market Place.

1. Anthony Norris' drawing of St Benet's abbey. Although this looks like an accurate drawing, it is not: the church had a west tower as well as the central one and no aisles to the nave. (NRO, RYE 6)

Another Saxon monastery was that of St Benet's at Holme founded in 800 AD. Like Dereham it developed around a site where a hermit lived. It was not a Benedictine institution, although the small church at which the hermits worshipped was dedicated to him (Benet is just a variation of Benedict). The site was destroyed by the Danes in 870. It was reoccupied by a group of hermits in the later tenth century. In 1019 the community was endowed with

The Beginnings

land by King Canute and formally became a Benedictine monastery. According to John Oxenedes, a chronicler who was a monk at St Benet's, the first church was of mud or clay (he uses the Latin word LUTEA: Joan Snelling's guide to the site wrongly translates this as 'timber'). It was later rebuilt in stone: this must have been brought here by boat, like the stone for Norwich cathedral. Lead roofs were added to the church and cloister buildings during the time of Abbot Ralph (1187-1210), according to William Worcester, who visited the monastery in the fifteenth century. A small house - also Benedictine - was founded at Thetford in 1020. This was not an independent monastery but a *cell*, or dependent house founded by a parent monastery from which it was administered. The parent house in this case was the great Benedictine abbey at Bury St Edmunds. The only other apparently pre-conquest monastery in Norfolk to survive into the Middle Ages was Molycourt, in the parish of Outwell. The date and circumstances of the foundation of this small and isolated house are not known. Blomefield is our authority for its being a Saxon house: he calls it 'this little old priory founded in the time of the Saxons (it is said)'. The earliest documentary reference to it comes from the early thirteenth century. Although the monastic site itself was in Norfolk, most of its property was across the county border in Cambridgeshire.

THE MONKS

As we have seen there were a small number of Saxon religious houses in Norfolk but the great age of monasticism was in the two centuries following the Norman Conquest of 1066. In 1066 there were 61 monastic houses in England with 1,200 inhabitants. In 1216 there were 700 houses with over 11,000 inhabitants. East Anglia and Norfolk played its part in this increase and more - whereas in 1066 only 3% of English monasteries were in East Anglia the figure for 1216 was no less than 10%.

The Conquest brought to England men who were used to the idea of founding large Benedictine monasteries. They saw the foundation of a religious house or the support of a hermit as a concrete act towards the salvation of their own souls and the souls of their relatives. This was an era when everyone believed in the power of the living to intercede for the dead by pilgrimages and by the saying of masses for their souls. This was the prime function of a monastery: its other activities such as alms giving, hospitality and schooling were very much secondary to the continuous round of prayer that took place within its walls.

It took a generation or so for the Normans to feel sufficiently secure in their English estates to found monasteries. First in Norfolk was Binham, founded

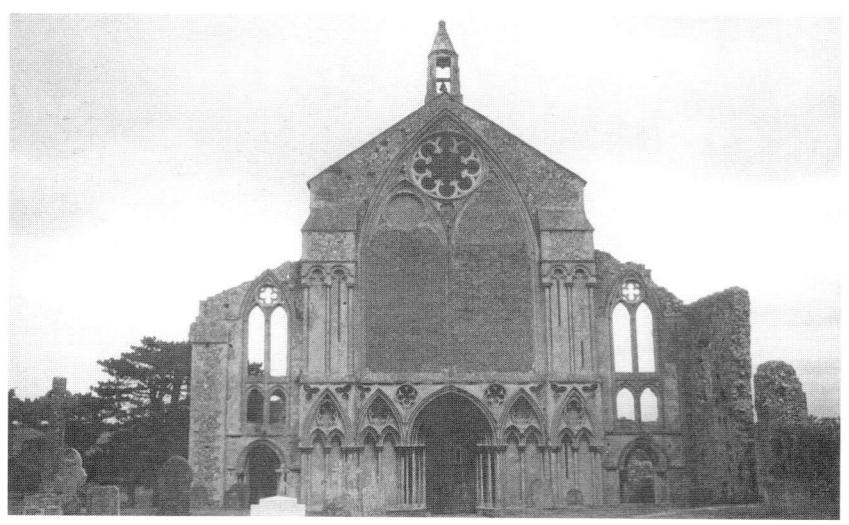

2. Binham priory: the west front

in about 1091 by Peter de Valoines. This was followed by Norwich, founded by Herbert Losinga in 1096: this was a cathedral as well as a monastery and is considered later. Robert de Caen founded the monastery at Horsham St Faith in 1105-6, and Wymondham was founded by William d'Albini in 1107: d'Albini, was chief butler to Henry I and lord of the manor of Wymondham. William's brother Richard was abbot of St Albans so it was natural for William to found his religious house as a daughter house of St Albans. Wymondham did not become an independent abbey until 1448. William and his wife Maud were buried before the high altar. In 1834 a vault was uncovered near the high altar: two lead coffins were found containing a woman and a prematurely born child, both embalmed. Maud is known to have died in childbirth so these bodies were probably the founder's wife and child.

A total of nine Benedictine male monasteries were founded in Norfolk after the Conquest. The only Benedictine female religious house was that at Carrow, just outside Norwich. This was, in one sense, of even higher status than the male houses: it was a royal foundation, being established by Stephen in 1146.

3. The Bucks' view of Wymondham abbey (NRO,MS 4579)

Each of these houses was an independent monastery except for Wymondham and Horsham St Faith. The latter was an *alien priory*, being actually owned and administered by a foreign religious house, in this case by the abbey of Conques in France. The reason for this illustrates some interesting aspects of medieval piety. Robert Fitzwalter was lord of the manor of Horsham and

Horstead. He and his wife Sybilla went on pilgrimage to Rome. On their way back they were robbed and imprisoned. They prayed for help from St Faith and she appeared to them in a vision and freed them, setting them on the way to her shrine at Conques (St Faith was an Aquitaine martyr, executed in about 287 AD. The fact that they prayed to her for help shows that the couple must already have had a special devotion to this saint). On reaching Conques they vowed to found a monastery on their English estates and brought two of the monks of Conques with them back to England. They began to build the monastery at Horsford but every night - so the story goes - devils destroyed the work of the previous day. Realising the futility of trying to continue, Robert and Sybilla abandoned the site and built the house at Horsham instead: there was no further devilry and the monastery was completed peacefully. To us this story may seem a mixture of sense and superstition but to the eleventh century mind it was eminently reasonable. It was told in a series of paintings in the monastery dining room, most of which still survive.

As has been said, Norwich Benedictine Priory had a special status as it was also the Cathedral church of the diocese. This was a combination characteristic of Norman England. Only one or two examples are known in Europe but in England of the seventeen medieval Cathedrals no less than nine were monastic (if we count Bath, which was a cathedral between 1090 and 1218, and shared the honour with Wells after that date). The idea cannot be called a success. Although the bishop was the titular abbot he became increasingly separated from the monastery and involved in affairs of the diocese and of state. The head of the monastic institution was the prior and there were often petty disputes between the bishop and the priory about rights to the Cathedral church. In Norwich the bishop had his own palace on the north side of the Cathedral and never lived within the priory itself, which was on the opposite side of the church.

Although Herbert was close to his monks, his successor Everard was not a monk at all, but a married man with children. After him the monks were able to choose their own prior, William Turbe, as bishop. He was to be one of the last direct links between the priory and the Cathedral. On his death John of Oxford became bishop: he was involved in several disputes with his own monks about rights and privileges. He was followed by John de Gray who was one of the king's servants and justices and as such was almost never in Norwich. The next bishop was Pandulph, an Italian who seems only to have visited the diocese twice. Only two more priors of Norwich Cathedral were to become bishop: Roger de Scarning who became bishop in 1266, and Alexander de Tottington who became bishop in 1407. All the other bishops

4. Interior of Norwich Cathedral priory, showing monks' stalls. (NRO, from MC 186/84)

were chosen by the monarch of the day. Many of these men had little connection with Norwich and virtually no contact with the Cathedral priory. The abbot's deputy, the prior, was the head of the house for all practical purposes. He too was an important dignitary and he had his own house to the east of the main cloister: this house is now the deanery.

The Benedictines constantly had to struggle to keep their standards high. The fourth Lateran Council of 1215 established a system of a yearly assembly of Benedictine abbots: after 1336 they met once every three years instead. In 1336, also, the Benedictines were formally allowed to eat meat on four days a week (Sunday, Monday, Tuesday and Thursday) except during the four weeks of advent and the nine weeks between Septuagesima and Easter. From the fourteenth century there was a tendency for monks to have their own money and increasing privacy. As early as the thirteenth century monks were being given 'pocket money' for spending on alms and small personal needs. This and a clothing allowance spread in the fourteenth century and monks began to receive fees for offices they held and for charities they said as well. In 1421 the order again tried reform. Payment of clothing and other allowances to individual monks was abolished. A monk's dress was to be uniform and simple. Private cells were forbidden.

Founding a Benedictine house was only one among a number of alternatives for a religiously minded landowner. The history of monasticism is really that of a series of waves of reforming ideals, each of which gradually lapsed into relative comfort. Most of these movements drew their inspiration directly from the rule of St Benedict: they thought it had become too lax in the Benedictine houses and they tried to restore it to its original purity. Of course much had changed since the time of St Benedict: he had envisaged a rural and largely uneducated community within the monastery. However by the tenth century the Benedictine monasteries had become victims of their own success. People found their style of living attractive and chose to give them money and land. Gradually the monks had become a wealthy spiritual elite, not so much 'slaves of God' as 'soldiers for Christ'.

The first of these reforming movements sprang from the abbey of *Cluny* in France. Cluny was founded in 910 as a Benedictine monastery but oneobserving the Benedictine Rule in the strictest sense. It was intended from the first to be a model of monastic virtue that others would want to copy. In order not to be at the mercy of the whims of individual founders of houses the order was placed directly under the control of the papacy. Unlike the Benedictine houses, which were independent of each other, all the Cluniac houses were under a centralised organisation, at the head of which was the

The monks

abbot of Cluny. The monks in all Cluniac houses took their vows of obedience to him in person and he appointed the prior, or head, of each Cluniac house. Their main aim was prayer and the glory of God. As R. H. C. Davis puts it: *'the prime purpose of [Cluniac] monks was not to educate other monks, nor to copy out the classics, nor to write history, nor to give hospitality, nor to tend the sick, nor to preach to the world, though some of these might well be by-products of their vocation. Their purpose was to live Christian life themselves. Seven times a day, and at midnight too, the praises of God were sung. At least 42 psalms were chanted every day and the whole life of the monastery centred on the church services. Those who were converted to Religion were not social workers looking for a job. They were inspired with the desire not to reform the world (for that was impossible) but to reform themselves'.*

The Cluniac reform movement spread throughout Europe - eventually nearly 1,500 monasteries came under their control. The first in Norfolk was at Castle Acre. The story of its foundation is a typical one. The lord of Castle Acre was William de Warenne and he and his wife visited Cluny. They found there 'such great holiness and religion and charity' that they asked the abbot, Hugh, if they could bring back some of the monks to their castle at

5. Castle Acre: the west front (NRO, from MC186/84)

Lewes and found a monastery there. Warenne founded Castle Acre from his Lewes monastery in 1085 - at first it was actually within the castle itself but it was soon moved to its present site. As anyone who has seen the glorious west front of the church can testify, they believed in celebrating God with beautiful architecture.

Further houses in Norfolk were founded from Castle Acre, including Bromholme, which became one of the most visited monasteries in England because of its relics, discussed later. The other major Cluniac house in Norfolk, founded directly from Cluny, was that at Thetford. It was established by Roger Bigot in 1104. He did this in lieu of making a pilgrimage to the Holy Land to which he had pledged himself. The site turned out to be too cramped and in 1107 it was moved. Roger Bigot was dying by then: he lived only long enough to lay the foundation stone of the new house. Within a week he was dead. He is supposed to have wanted burial in his priory but Herbert Losinga managed to have the body buried in the Cathedral monastery in Norwich. However when the dispute came to court, Herbert produced many witnesses to say that Roger had wished to be buried in the cathedral: although the monks of Thetford had documentary evidence in their favour this was presumably forged and Herbert won the case.

Descendants of founders would continue to act as patrons. William de Lesewys founded the small Cluniac house of Normansburgh on his estate at South Raynham. He gave them 76 acres of land. His son Godefrid gave them further pieces of land and made the house a cell of Castle Acre - the divine offices were to be celebrated at Normansburgh by at least three monks from the mother house. He gave them the church of South Raynham and nine acres of land and also two 'serfs' - Richard Shepherd 'with all his brood' and John Le Frere 'with all his brood and also the tenement which he owes me'.

Normansburgh had possessions in just five parishes. There was a small Cluniac house at Slevesholm in Methwold and another at Heacham: the latter was founded directly from Lewes and was little more than a *grange*, or centre from which the monastic estates were run.

The English Cluniac houses gradually broke free from control by the mother house in France - Thetford, for example, secured a papal bull allowing them to elect their own prior some time before 1376.

Another major reforming movement was that of the *Cistercians*. This began when a group of monks left their monastery at Molesmes for Citeaux in 1098. They also tried to go back to a strict form of the Benedictine rule, rejecting

The monks

6. Bromholme priory: the ivy has since been cleared from the ruins (NRO, MC 365/2)

all personal possessions such as 'coats, capes, worsted cloth, hoods, pants, combs, counterpanes and bedclothes'. The refusal to wear underpants was the object of much scorn by their enemies. They did not want to live off other people's labour so they did not own manors, tithes or rents. They stressed the need for simple, plain churches with no silverware or fancy decoration. They went back to the ideal of monks doing manual work and also brought a new innovation into the monastic scheme of things: the lay-brother. These took vows, but were not ordained and were not usually literate. They in effect did most of the manual work in the monastery and on its estates, which in Benedictine and Cluniac houses was done by tenants or by hired servants. However the monks did manual work too, at least in the beginning. Lay brothers were not always a success - they could be unruly and difficult to manage. By the fourteenth century it was found better to rent out the land or have the work done by hired servants.

Like Cluny the Cistercian houses were directly under papal control and organised from the centre. However the abbot of Citeaux was not a dictator in the way that the abbot of Cluny was - he himself was subject to the control of the 'chapter-general' - the meeting of all the abbots of the houses of the Order.

The Cistercians, too, were a great success: by 1153 the house had over 300 daughter-houses. Some of the most famous ruined abbeys of England that people can visit today are Cistercian, such as Fountains, Rievaulx and Tintern. However they preferred wild out-of-the-way places and Norfolk was probably too tame for them. The only Cistercian house in Norfolk was the female one at Marham: this is considered in the chapter on Nuns in this book. There were some small cells, however, dependent on Cistercian monasteries elsewhere: Mount Grace in Field Dalling was a cell of the French house of Savigny and Prior's Thorns in Swaffham was a cell of Sawtry in Huntingdonshire.

The popularity of the Cistercians was again to some extent their own undoing. Within 50 years of their foundation people were complaining of the wealth of their monasteries and the greed of their monks.

One other group of reforming monks should be mentioned for completeness - the *Carthusians*. They were founded by Bruno at La Chartreuse in 1084 and adopted a very strict interpretation of the rule of St Benedict with a return to the anchorite ideal. Each monk had his own cell where he prayed, worked and ate. They met together only for certain church services. The order had a very high reputation, which it maintained right down to the Dissolution. However they founded no houses in Norfolk and do not feature any more in this book.

Many of the Norman landowners in England still held lands in France. One reflection of the close connection between the two countries is the way in which several French monasteries were given estates in England. Some times they established a small cell on the estate, thus forming an alien priory, similar in status to Horsham St Faith but on a very much smaller scale: the house might well be staffed by only two or three monks, chosen on a rotational basis from the monks of the mother-house in France. On other occasions, the monastery could just act as landowner, making money out of the estate but not actually having a cell there. The distinction is not always clear. Taylor's *Index Monasticus* refers to alien priories at Costessy and West Wretham, for example, but I have not included these in the list at the end of this book: they appear to have been estates rather than cells. On the other hand, I have followed Taylor and included Horstead and Field Dalling as alien priories, although the Ordnance Survey's map of *Monastic Britain* regards them as merely granges.

Other groups of people who chose to live together as a community bound by a rule were technically not **monks** but **canons**. They are discussed in the next chapter.

THE CANONS

The word 'canon' has several different meanings in church circles. Here we are talking about priests who chose to follow the example of the apostles and live a communal life without any personal possessions. St Augustine in the early fifth century had recommended that all priests should live in this way. The life-style was adopted by many groups of priests serving large churches, which often acquired the name 'minster'. They lived in collegiate houses and drew their stipend from a common fund. However they did not take a vow of poverty or of obedience to any rule of conduct. In 1069 the Lateran Council urged them to bind themselves to following a particular rule, like monastic communities. Some chose not to do this: these became known as *secular canons* and are not the concern of this book (a good Norfolk example of such a group is that based on Attleborough parish church). Others did choose to follow a rule: they are known as regular canons. The rule chosen was not that of St Benedict but that of St Augustine: they are therefore known as Augustinian or Austin canons, but are more commonly called black canons from the colour of their robes. Technically this was not a rule as such but an adaptation of advice given in a letter by St Augustine to his sister who was a nun. Each house added its own customs to this, so they varied very much in the actual details of their practices. In general the customs were deliberately moderate in their demands. As a canon of Barnwell, Cambridgeshire, wrote *'Like a kind master he [Augustine] did not drive his apostles with a rod of iron, but invited those who love the beauty of holiness to the door of salvation with a moderate rule'*. The canons always had meat several days a week, and the rules of silence were less severe than in monastic houses.

A very large number of houses of black canons were founded in England from the early twelfth century onwards. They were popular because they were much cheaper to found than Benedictine houses and also because the canons were more involved in community life than monks. They were all priests and often served as parish priests in the churches given to them. They also ran schools and hospitals. There were just over twenty houses of black canons in Norfolk (including those that were cells to larger houses elsewhere). There was also an Austin nunnery at Crabhouse in Wiggenhall St Mary Magdalen, considered later. Here we concentrate on four of the houses, Westacre, Walsingham, Creake and Weybourne, as examples of the different ways in which houses of regular canons might develop.

Westacre originated as a community of priests serving in and around the parish church of All Saints. They became formalised into a group of regular canons in the early twelfth century. Their foundation charter says *'the life which they adopted is such as can be found in the Acts of the Apostles - the multitude of them that believed were of one heart and of one soul: neither said any of them ought of the things which he possessed was his own: but they had all things common'*. The charter tells us that one of the canons was a married priest with a son. He had obviously become convinced of the claims of clerical celibacy as he now decided to follow a celibate life in communion with like-minded canons. The community formally became an Austin priory in the 1130s or 1140s.

Walsingham was to become the most famous and most visited Austin priory in the country and perhaps in Europe. The priory as such dates from about 1155 but the site had already been a revered one for almost a century. In 1061 a lady called Richeldis had had a vision of the Holy House in Nazareth where the Annunciation had taken place and where Jesus had been brought up.

7. Walsingham priory: the east end of the church (NRO, MC 530/2)

The canons

The Virgin Mary appeared and ordered Richeldis to build an exact replica of the house on her lands in Walsingham. It was decided to build it between two holy wells there: however when craftsmen tried to build the house they ran into problems. On arriving for work the following day they found that the foundations they had begun had been moved 200 yards during the night and that the house had been miraculously completed to a perfection they could never have achieved. This shrine became known as the Chapel of Our Lady of Walsingham.

The Holy House made Walsingham one of the most popular places of pilgrimage in the Christian world. These pilgrims included almost every king of England. Edward I was especially keen because of an incident that had happened in one of his palaces when he was a young man. He was playing chess with a knight when he left the table for a short while (to relieve himself perhaps?). At that moment a huge stone fell from the ceiling on the very spot where he had been sitting: Edward attributed this miracle to Our Lady of Walsingham. At Walsingham itself, the sub-prior was miraculously saved after he had tumbled into one of the holy wells. In 1513 Arthur Plantagenet, the illegitimate son of Edward IV and an admiral of the English fleet, was saved by Our Lady of Walsingham. He was in a ship that, under full sail, ran into a rock off the French coast. Arthur called out to Our Lady, promising he would not eat flesh or fish until he visited her: this did the trick and the ship was saved. All the people who had experienced the grace and favour of Our Lady of Walsingham naturally visited the house and made gifts in gratitude. The house had several important relics, which are considered later. Erasmus described Walsingham as *'the seat of the Gods, so bright and shining it is all over with jewels, gold and silver'*.

8. Creake abbey: the chancel, transepts and chapels, taken from the site of the nave

The abbey at Creake began as a family chapel for the Nerfords founded in about 1206.

It was elevated into a hospital by Alice de Nerford in gratitude for her nephew's naval victory over theFrench in 1217: her nephew was the justiciar Hubert de Burgh and as the battle took place on St Bartholomew's Day he was naturally chosen as patron saint of the hospital. It was a successful venture: in 1226 the Archbishop of York granted an indulgence for those who gave to it and commented that many needy folk went there and very great misery was alleviated. About ten years later the hospital became a priory. This was a common progression: four other Norfolk Austin houses - Wormegay, Peterstone, Hempton and Great Massingham - had begun as hospitals.

9. Weybourne priory

10. Beeston priory: the chancel

Weybourne priory was founded in about 1200 by the local lord of the manor, Sir Ralph Mainwaring. It eventually had property in 30 Norfolk parishes as well as the churches of Weybourne, Colkirk and East Beckham. It was always a small and poor house, but lived up to its founder's intentions in that its churches were not just sources of income: for example one of the canons served the church of East Beckham, four miles away.

Some of the Norfolk houses of Austin canons were not part of the main stream of the order. Beeston, Peterstone, Massingham and

The canons 21

11. The church of the canons of the Holy Sepulchre at Thetford, the only surviving building in England of this order of canons.

Weybridge formed a group of houses of Austin canons which had a special status: they were not subject to the General Chapter of the order but an independent grouping, known as the Order of Peterstone. Their prime purpose seems to have been to house travellers, especially perhaps pilgrims visiting Walsingham. They were all very remote - the friar John Capgrave described them in a sermon *'not in the world, as they say, but in Northfolk'*.

Another unusual house was that of the canons of the Holy Sepulchre in Thetford. This order was founded in 1114 to help pilgrims travelling to the shrine of the Holy Sepulchre in Jerusalem, built on the supposed site of Jesus' burial. They followed the rule of St Augustine. Their house in Thetford was founded by William de Warenne, who was himself to be killed on the Second Crusade in 1148. The order had only six houses in England and this is the only one of which there are any remains.

As with the monks, so there were reforming movements among canons too. In 1120 a canon called Norbert founded a house at Prémontré in France. The name Prémontré itself had an interesting origin, illustrative of the way of thinking of the time. Norbert was a Black Canon who had left the order and become a wandering preacher. One day he was granted - by the grace of Our Lady he was convinced - a vision of canons dressed in white, carrying crosses and lights, walking around a valley. In 1121 he was travelling in Northern France when he recognised the site of his vision. He built his monastery here and called it pré montré - the pre-shown. He dedicated it to Our Lady and his canons' devotions stressed the cult of Mary in all their rituals. The white canons in England at first paid money to their head house at Prémontré: this was forbidden during the French Wars. In 1512 the abbey of Welbeck was made the English head house of the Order.

White canons followed the rule of St Augustine but added some of the customs of the Cistercian monks to create a way of life more austere than that of the black canons. They were called the Premonstratensian Canons after the name of their first house but are more generally known as white canons from the colour of their robes. The white canons had three houses in Norfolk. The first, West Dereham, was founded in 1188 by Hubert Fitzwalter, the Archbishop of Canterbury, who was a native of the town. Langley was founded ten years later and Wendling much later, in about 1267. Wendling was founded by the local landowner Robert de Stuteville and was to be the last house of the order established in England. Fashions in religious piety in medieval England were continuously changing: sometimes Norfolk was in the forefront of fashion, at other times -as in this case - it lagged behind nationatrends. All white canons were priests and they very often served as parish priests in their churches - the canons of Langley were serving half a dozen local churches in the fifteenth century and those of West Dereham were serving four.

Another group of canons was that founded by St Gilbert of Sempringham. He has the distinction of being the only Englishman to found an order. The order was also the only one to include both men and women within the same house. Gilbert was the parish priest at Sempringham in Lincolnshire. He built a small convent close to his church at the request of seven women of the parish in 1131. The movement was a local one: in his lifetime Gilbert founded 13 houses (nine double ones and four for canons only). Almost all were in Lincolnshire and Yorkshire. Gilbert died in 1189, aged about 105. After his death a few more houses were founded, but only one double house. This was at Shouldham and became one of the most important houses of the order. Gilbert would have liked his houses to become part of the Cistercian order, but they would not allow this. Pope Eugenius III urged him to regard his group of houses as an order in its own right. Gilbert then developed his own system: the nuns were to follow the rule of St Benedict, the canons that of St Augustine. The houses also had lay brothers and sisters: they followed the rule of the Cistercians. The Gilbertines had in effect two monastic communities - for the nuns and the canons - built around one church. The church had a wall in it running down the middle so that the nuns and canons could share in the service but not actually see each other.

THE MILITARY ORDERS

The military orders embraced an idea most people of the twentieth century find strange - the church at war. They were made up of men dedicated to fighting for their God, yet they were also monks, taking the monastic vows and living a common life. They were not ordained because priests were not allowed to carry arms (and therefore they needed chaplains to administer the sacraments and hear their confessions). Their main sphere of activity was in the Holy Land where they became increasingly involved in military activity against the Saracens. Later they fought against Muslims in Spain and eventually even against other Christians who were deemed to be heretics. Their houses in England were really collecting points for money to fund their military campaigns.

Four groups of these military orders had a presence in Norfolk. The most well known are probably the *Templars* or *Knights of the Temple of Solomon in Jerusalem.* After the crusaders captured Jerusalem in 1099 - incidentally murdering every Moslem and every Jew in the city apart from the governor - most of them went home. Only 500 knights remained in the Holy Land. The Templars originated from a group of nine knights (almost all French) formed in 1115 by Hugue de Payens and Godfrey de Saint Adhemar. In 1118 they swore an oath before the Patriarch of Jerusalem to protect pilgrims and to observe the monastic vows of poverty, chastity and obedience. They were originally called the Poor Knights of Christ but King Baldwin gave them quarters in his palace in Jerusalem. This was thought to be on the site of Solomon's Temple, hence the name Templars.

12. Ingham church: the sacrist lived in the uper storey of the porch

In 1124 Hugue came to Europe to seek help in forming a rule. He met Bernard of Clairvaux, the leading light of the Cistercian movement. Bernard became a great supporter of the knights and the rule they adopted was based on the Cistercian rule. He justified their aims in this way - *'they fear not the sin of killing an enemy or the peril of their own death, in as much as death either inflicted or borne for Christ has no taint of crime and rather merits the greater glory'*. He praised them in terms that probably also expressed the things he disliked about relative 'softies' in the monastic world such as Benedictine monks and Austin canons: *'Imprudent words, senseless occupations, immoderate laughter, whispering or even suppressed giggling are unknown. They have a horror of chess and dice; they hate hunting; they don't even enjoy the flight of the falcon. They despise mimes, jugglers, story-tellers, dirty songs, entertainments of buffoons - all these they regard as vanities and mere follies. They cut their hair short because they know it is shameful for a man to wear it long. Never overdressed they bathe rarely and are dirty and hirsute, tanned by the coat of mail and the sun'*. The knights took part in many battles in the Holy Land as the Moslems gradually regained ground. Jerusalem was lost in 1243 and after 1289 only Acre remained in Christian hands. This city finally fell in 1291, with the death of many Templars: some 20,000 Templars had died altogether in battle in the Holy Land.

Their houses in England and elsewhere in Europe were intended to recruit and train new members and also to administer the properties they owned - at its height the order owned over 9,000 manors throughout Europe. The Templars had just one house in Norfolk, at Haddiscoe. The date of foundation is not known but it was certainly before 1218.

Some people blamed the military orders for the loss of the Holy Land. The Templars were accused of black magic and other offences but were found innocent in several countries including England. However the King of France, Philip, was determined to have them dissolved and he persuaded the Pope to suppress the order in 1312. Their properties were supposed to be given to the Hospitallers but this often never happened and they were in effect seized and kept by local or national officials. In Norfolk the sheriff seized the possessions of Haddiscoe and they appear to have remained in his hands and those of his successor.

Another military order was that of the *Hospitallers* or *Knights of St John of Jerusalem.* The Hospitallers originated in a hospice for pilgrims founded near the Holy Sepulchre in Jerusalem by a group of merchants from Amalfi in Italy. This was founded in 1070, when Jerusalem was still in Moslem hands.

After Jerusalem fell it became a hospital to care for sick crusaders and pilgrims. The knights originally followed the Benedictine Rule but in 1113 adopted that of St Augustine instead. By 1126 they were a military order, at first to defend their hospitals but later they were given many of the great crusader castles of the Holy Land including the greatest of them all, Krak des Chevaliers, which did not fall to the Moslems until 1271. As the Templars wore a red cross on their robes, the Hospitallers chose to wear a white cross.

In 1256 the Templars and Hospitallers actually fought against each other when they took different sides in the wars between Genoese and Venetians in Acre, and the knights began killing each other. However both groups fought together in the fall of Acre where many knights of both orders were killed. Soon afterwards the Hospitallers took over the Island of Rhodes which did not fall to the Moslems until 1522.

Like the Templars, the Hospitallers had only one house in Norfolk: theirs was at Carbrooke. Roger, Earl of Clare, founded it shortly before 1173. The Countess of Clare founded a small house for sisters of the order at the same place but this was short lived. In 1180 all the sisters of the order were grouped together in one house at Buckland in Somerset. The houses in Europe were called Commanderies and served the same purposes as those of the Templars. They were active money collectors too and they employed four clerks to go around Norfolk raising money. Income from these collections averaged over £80 a year, a large sum for the time. There are two coffin lids in Carbrooke church which are probably those of the Countess of Clare and one of her sons: if so, they are the earliest identifiable tombs in any Norfolk church. Although they do not actually give names, the identification seems fairly certain: the inscription on one stone translates as:

Here lies buried a mother of the family of Clare by a soldier of which [family] England boasts herself renowned.

It is an interesting question whether the coffin lids have always been within the parish church, or whether they were removed from the preceptory at the Dissolution: we shall see several examples of the migration of monuments later in this book.

A third military order was the *Order of St Lazarus*. They ran a hospital for lepers just outside the wall of Jerusalem. They followed the Augustine Rule. They never became a purely military order like the other two - they never had very many knights and continued to exercise duties of helping lepers. After the fall of Acre they moved to Cyprus and soon afterwards abandoned their military activities. The order had a single house in Norfolk, at Choseley on the hills just behind the north west coast of the county: it was founded by Walter Gifford, Earl of Buckingham, in the reign of Henry I. They also had a cell at Westwade, outside Wymondham, which had originally been founded as a leper hospital by William d'Albini. Westwade was bought by Robert Kett after the Dissolution. It was forfeited to the Crown at the time of his execution for rebellion in 1549 but later restored to the Kett family. There was later a Quaker meeting house of the Society of Friends on the site: a second Quaker house built close by can still be seen. There are about a dozen manors in Norfolk with the name 'Chossels': this is a corruption of the word 'Choseley' and indicates that the manor was once part of the property of this monastic house.

The final military order with a Norfolk presence was the *Order of the Holy Trinity and St Victor for the Redemption of Captives.* The main function of this group was to ransom Christians captured by the Saracens. The head house of the order was Ingham, which was also their only house in the county: it was founded by Sir Miles Stapeleton in 1360. The prior had care of the college while the sacrist looked after the parishoners and administered to them in the nave of the church. He lived in the room above the porch of the church that can still be seen, although the remainder of the monastic buildings have largely disappeared. The house was a popular one and received several gifts of land in the later fourteenth century.

13. Remains of the cloister on the north side of Ingham church

THE NUNS

The history of female religious houses has been largely neglected by historians over the years: the classic work on Monastic Orders by Dom. Knowles almost ignores the subject. Nunneries are still often thought of as little more than residences of daughters of upper-class families who had failed to find themselves husbands. Fortunately recent work on the houses in Norwich diocese by Marilyn Oliva has redressed the balance and brought to light a level of devoted service at least as high as that in the male religious houses.

The number of nuns in Norfolk was always far less than that of their male counterparts. There were just six nunneries in the county - at Carrow, Thetford, Blackborough, Marham, Shouldham and Crabhouse. The average number of nuns at each house was between eight and twelve so there were about 50 nuns in Norfolk at any one time.

The nunneries fell into two broad types - urban ones at Carrow and Thetford, rural ones (all in the Nar Valley) at the other four places.

Carrow Priory (Norfolk people insist on calling it Carrow Abbey) is unique in its status among these houses because it was a royal foundation. The original grant was made by King Stephen in 1146. It appears that two of the first nuns had formerly been sisters at the -otherwise unknown - hospital of St Mary and St John in Norwich. This was followed by grants from several landed gentry families so that by 1291 it had possessions in 75 parishes in Norfolk and two in Suffolk. The church here was the largest in Norwich apart from the cathedral itself.

Because Carrow was just outside the city walls of Norwich there were continual disputes between it and the city authorities as to whether the priory fell within the city's jurisdiction. The most dramatic of these came in 1416. In that year William Koc of Trowse was set upon by seven men armed with spades and sticks and beaten to death. Koc's widow Margery knew the names of the murderers and accused the prioress of Carrow, Edith, of harbouring them. The case turned on whether the city or the county authorities should try the gang members and at one stage Edith and another nun were arrested and charged with the murders themselves! They were eventually acquitted.

The other urban female religious house was that at Thetford. The Saxon monastery already mentioned had declined until in about 1160 there were

14. Modern house built in the remnants of Thetford nunnery

only two monks here. It was decided to withdraw them to the parent house at Bury St Edmunds and to fill the house with a group of nuns living at Lyng. Like Carrow, Thetford was outside the main town - there was thus a strong element of seclusion even in the urban nunneries. Thetford was physically dependent on Bury St Edmunds - every week supplies of cooked meat, along with 35 loaves and 96 gallons of beer were sent from Bury to the nunnery along twelve miles of poor road. The supply wagons were obvious targets for robbers and the food did not always arrive in a satisfactory state: in 1361 they were replaced with an annual supply of corn and barley from the parent house.

The four houses along the Nar Valley were probably founded there precisely because it was one of the most isolated and wild parts of the county. Although each was part of a different order they share the same pattern of being endowed with a small amount of poor-quality land, perhaps just in their parish and one or two neighbouring ones. The cartulary of Crabhouse specifically says that it was begun by a female hermit called Lena '*a maiden whose heart the Holy Spirit moved to seek a decent place where she might serve God without disturbance, found the place called Crabhouse all wild and far around on every side was no human habitation*'. She attracted followers but a flood forced them to abandon the site. One of the sisters then lived as a hermit in the nearby churchyard of Wiggenhall St Mary Magdalen until the house was refounded. This story of the nunnery's origin comes from the fourteenth century cartulary and may not be completely historically accurate. However it shows how the nuns themselves thought of the history of their house. Crabhouse was definitely established as an Austin nunnery by the early thirteenth century.

The history of Crabhouse demonstrates how monks, priests and nuns could co-operate when the need arose. The early nuns appear to have been supported in some way by the monks of Castle Acre: in the 1180s it was agreed that deceased nuns should be buried at Castle Acre priory cemetery. Later, John Wiggenhall, abbot of West Dereham in the fifteenth century, was a great supporter of Crabhouse nunnery: Joan Wiggenhall, the prioress there, was his cousin and both his parents were buried there. Abbot John helped provide images for the nunnery church. Another cousin of Joan's was Edmund Perys, the parson at Watlington. He had helped pay for work on the chancel of the nun's church in the 1420s. Perys died in 1427 and left a will expressing his wish to be buried at the nunnery.

The early history of Blackborough is also obscure. It was founded in about 1150 by Roger de Scales and his wife Muriel as a house for Benedictine monks. Within a few years it seems to have been devoted to the support of religious of both sexes and by 1200 it was assigned for the use of Benedictine nuns. The Scales family maintained an interest in Blackborough for several generations. One of their sons, William, entered the community in 1160. Another son, Robert, made grants of land, and so did his sons a generation later. In 1238 a woman named Katherine de Scales was the prioress: no doubt she was yet another member of the family.

At the end of the twelfth century the Gilbertines came to the Nar Valley. We have already described this order, unique in having both male and females within one monastery - in different groups of buildings of course. The Gilbertine house at Shouldham was founded by Geoffrey Fitzpiers, the chief justice of England, at the time of Richard the Lionheart (1189-1199). He founded the house for the souls of his late master, King Henry (Richard's father), and also that of his wife Beatrice who had died in childbirth. She had been buried at the priory of Chicksands in Bedfordshire. Geoffrey had her body dug up and brought to Shouldham where she was reburied. When Geoffrey himself died in 1212 he was buried beside her. Geoffrey also granted to this priory twelve shops in London: these were rented out to raise money which, according to the charter, was to go to sustain the lights of the church and to provide sacramental wine.

15 Marham abbey showing the line of the cloister roof with the rose windows above

The last nunnery to be established in the Nar Valley was the Cistercian one at Marham. The growth of the Cistercian Order and its love of isolated country sites has already been discussed. Isabel, widow of Hugh Albini, Earl of Arundel, founded a female Cistercian house at Marham in 1249. It was established for the good of the souls of her father and mother and of her late husband. It was one of the very few female religious houses in England to be formally accepted into the Cistercian order and the only one to have the status of an abbey rather than a priory.

What did nuns actually do? Although, as we have seen, they came from four different orders - three Benedictine, one Austin, one Cistercian and one Gilbertine - the life styles were so similar that they can be discussed together. As with their male counterparts their main function was to pray and this took up most of their day. In an age when almost everyone believed in the power of prayer, this was an important and much-valued function. Foundation charters, as we have seen, sometimes specifically named the souls who were intended to be helped by prayer. Many people left money in their wills to the female religious houses, often with specific requests that prayers be said for them on the anniversaries of their death. One sign of the general popularity of

The nuns 31

the nunneries is that people continued to leave money to them right up to the Dissolution, even after support of this kind for the richer abbeys and priories had waned.

Another function of the female religious house was in education. Unfortunately this is very poorly recorded. Lady Julian, Norwich anchorite, and the writer of *Visions of Divine Love* may have been educated at Carrow. There is no direct evidence for this: however St Julian's church where she lived belonged to Carrow priory, which was only a few hundred yards down King Street. It seems a reasonable assumption that she was educated at the nunnery: probably other local girls were taught there too.

One way in which the nunneries tended to be more a part of the local community that the male houses was that they usually shared their church with the local villagers. The churches of the Norfolk female religious houses were never parish churches as such - indeed at Marham the parish church was just across the road from the nuns' church. However they often seem to have become the church to which local people went by choice. It was quite common for lay people specifically to ask to be buried in the cemeteries of nunneries (this happened in the friary cemeteries as well, but much less often in those of monks and canons). The Marham cartulary lists the *mortuaries* or gifts to the abbey by sixteen people who wished to be buried in the nun's cemetery. Most gave gowns, some highly-coloured: Sir Ralph Hersent gave a violet one, for example, and Cecil Norburgh a gown with a collar of *miniver* fur (white fur from an ermine in its winter coat). Some people gave other things however - Thomas Rynstede's mortuary was a sorrel horse. A priest called John Champeney, who had lived at the abbey, left them a book. Presumably it was not to the nuns' taste as they promptly sold it for 15 marks.

Marilyn Oliva has looked at the status of the nuns. Surprisingly few - about 15% - are of the class of the country gentry or above (the highest in status of the Norfolk nuns was probably Margaret, daughter of the Earl of Warwick, who was a nun at Shouldham:

16. Nuns or donors? Skeletons in stone coffins found at Thetford nunnery in 1908 (NRO,MC 365/153)

when Warwick died in 1369 he left her a ring, a covered cup and 40 marks). By far the greatest number of nuns - about two thirds - were from the lower gentry, people concerned with parish rather than county or national affairs. In Norwich the city tradesmen and industrialists not surprisingly favoured Carrow Priory where many of their daughters were probably educated and some stayed to take up the religious life.

Like the monks (and with the same exceptions, referred to later) the nuns were regularly visited by diocesan officials. Most of the complaints were of a petty nature. Only one case of immorality occurs in all these records - a nun at Crabhouse had had a child by one of the local gentry (the child had since died). Other complaints were minor - in 1514 the nuns of Thetford uncharitably complained that they were afraid the prioress was about to admit as a nun one Dorothy Sturghis who was both deformed and deaf. Twelve years later some of the older nuns at Carrow were complaining that the services were being sung too fast - two also complained that the beer was too weak!

As with the male religious houses there were many other residents apart from the nuns. These were not always female. Long term guests of either sex might be attached to nunneries: in 1532 Thomas Foster was living at Thetford nunnery with his wife, three children and a maid. Children were living at the nunneries to be educated - they were supposed to be supported by their parents but it was not always easy to get the money. There were female servants of course - in 1537 there were four at Marham, eight at Blackborough and eight at Carrow. There were male servants too for the farm work - eight at Blackborough, seven at Carrow and two at Marham: these were often known as 'hinds'. As we have stressed, the nuns needed priests to administer the sacraments: in 1537 there was one priest at Blackborough and two at Carrow. If no priest could come to them they had to break their self-imposed rule of seclusion and go to the parish church as the nuns of Flixton, Suffolk, did in 1493 after their priest had broken his arm.

There are a small number of references in wills to nuns not living in any of the known female houses. In 1527 a man called Baldwin Dereham left money to nuns at West Dereham. This was a male house of white canons. However some houses of the white canons did start off as double houses so just possibly this was the case at West Dereham: if so this 1527 will is our only known documentary evidence for it. Baldwin left 10 shillings to the abbot and 10 shillings 'to be evenly divided between the chanons and nonnys there'. He also left money to Crabhouse and to a niece who was a nun at Shouldham so he clearly had a high regard for female monasticism. There are also references to nuns at Swaffham in 1242 and 1280, at 'Hengham' in 1385 and at 'Greencrofte' in 1280. Nothing at all is known about these people apart from the mentions in wills but clearly the testators thought of them both as being nuns and as worthy of bequests.

Other groups of women lived in small communities dedicated to religious service, but without taking formal vows and becoming nuns. Such groups are often known as *beguinages* after similar but larger groups that existed in the Low Countries: however this term is never used in medieval documents. In fact the only known references to such groups of women are in wills of people bequeathing them small sums of money. Four wills dated between about 1427 and 1444 mention a group of sisters dedicated to chastity living in a house in St Swithin's parish in Norwich. Another group of sisters, also dedicated to chastity, were living in a house in St Lawrence's parish between 1442 and 1472.

The most well-known of these groups is the one supposed to have lived in the fifteenth century house at the top of Elm Hill in Norwich, now called the Briton's Arms. Unfortunately there is no known surviving documentary evidence for their existence. However the eminent historian Francis Blomefield, writing in the eighteenth century mentions a group of sisters living under a religious vow at the north west corner of St Peter Hungate. He does not give a source for this information and none has ever been found: it seems most unlikely that he would have made it up, so presumably he is quoting from a now-lost document. (R. Taylor's *Index Monasticus* written in 1821 gives the same information but he probably just copied it from Blomefield's book). The strongest evidence for the existence of such a community is the nature of the building itself which is made up of individual 'bedsits', and which is indeed at the north west corner of St Peter Hungate churchyard.

17. The Briton's Arms in Norwich: a medieval beguinage?

Other women who did not wish to become nuns might express their religious convictions by taking certain vows, usually that of chastity. These 'vowesses' might continue to live within the community or might choose to isolate themselves from it to a greater or lesser extent. Our limited knowledge of them is derived from bequests in wills and from brasses in churches. Norfolk examples in wills include a vowess called Margaret, who was residing at Crabhouse nunnery in 1497, and Lady Dorothy Curson who was anchoress at Carrow in 1520. Brasses to vowesses are rare: Pevsner and Wilson say that only four are recorded in England. One is at Witton (near Norwich): there is a brass just inside the door to Juliana Anyell, 'vowess', of about 1500. The tiny church of Frenze has a brass to Joan Braham who must be of similar status - she is described on the brass as 'widow and dedicated to God'. These brasses are important as they show these ladies in the dress they would have worn in life - which appears, however, to be identical to that of any other widow of their time.

HERMITS AND ANCHORITES

A small number of people might find their devotion to God best expressed by a solitary life-style: these are usually called hermits or anchorites and more of these are known in Norwich (in the later Middle Ages at least) than from any other English city. They are known mainly from bequests left to them in wills. Some lived in small cells attached to churches, others lived on the city's gates and bridges and presumably played a part in maintaining these structures. There are references in deeds and wills to hermits in other Norfolk towns and also in the country: for example an anchorite at Ormesby is mentioned in the will of Oliver Wyth of 1291. There was a hermitage by the bridge at Downham Market in the time of King John. A deed of 1250 referring to land in nearby Bexwell mentions 'Amphelis the recluse': if this was the current hermit at the bridge the place must have been occupied for several generations. However the Norwich examples are better known as the documentary sources have been more thoroughly analysed.

Hermits and anchorites did not necessarily renounce all ownership of property. Some had servants as did Julian of Norwich - one of these later became an anchorite herself. At least three Norwich hermits left wills: Richard Ferneys hermit 'once of Newbridge' left money and possessions to churches and to other Norwich hermits. The other Norwich hermits leaving wills were Thomas Basset and John Knot. In general anchorites remained all their lives in the cell they had chosen, but hermits might travel. One Norwich citizen, Robert Baxter, left Ferneys £40 to make a pilgrimage for him to Jerusalem and to Rome: at the latter place he was to 'go round 15 times in a great circle', presumably a traditional pilgrim's ritual. Some of the anchorites were monks or friars who wished to push their religious devotion further than a normal communal life-style but others were priests or even lay-people. In theory they had to obtain a licence from the bishop and occasionally the issue of such licences can be found in the Bishop's registers.

Some women too chose to live a solitary life in an anchorage attached to a church or religious house. The names of between twelve and fifteen such women in Norwich are known from bequests in wills but there may have been others for whom no record has survived. The most famous one of course is Julian of Norwich. Julian was an anchoress at St Julian's church, Norwich: she took her name from the church not (as many suppose) the other way round. Her book - *Revelations of Divine Love* - has been described as the first major work in English by a woman. It is one of the most beautiful and moving books of devotion ever written. Male religious houses might have female anchorites within their precincts, as did the Dominican friary in Norwich and the Franciscan friary at Walsingham.

A few hermitages developed into religious houses, as happened at St Benet's. The site was first occupied by a hermit named Suneman in about 800. Followers gathered around him, living in huts but worshipping together in a small church. The site was destroyed by Danish invaders in 870: about a century later it was reoccupied by another hermit, Wolfric: he too attracted followers around him, from whom the monastery evolved. Crabhouse and at the Saxon nunnery at Dereham also developed from hermitages. Most hermitages, however, just died out, perhaps after a generation or two of use. Few physical remains survive of the buildings of hermits and anchorites. There is a small room built into the buttress of the tower of Walpole St Andrew church which could well be an anchorite's cell, although no documentary evidence exists for an anchorage here. The arch at the Whitefriars site in Norwich is also believed to be a remnant of a cell. On the north side of Blackfriars Hall the small window survives through which an anchorite in her cell could look into the friars' church and see the high altar. St Julian's cell, attached to the church in King Street in Norwich is a modern reconstruction. However it is probably the only place where one can experience today something of what an anchorite's life was like.

THE FRIARS

The arrival of the friars in England in the early thirteenth century had a tremendous impact on religious and social life in the country, yet today they are largely forgotten. Most people are uncertain as to the difference between a monk and a friar and would probably only know the names of two friars, one fictitious and the other world-famous but not thought of by most people as being a friar.

The fictitious one is of course Friar Tuck, the fat and jolly friend to Robin Hood, who shared Robin's adventures in Sherwood Forest and supported the interests of good King Richard against the schemes of his evil brother Prince John. There is an historical error in this legend unfortunately: no friar came to England until a quarter of a century after the death of King Richard.

The world-famous friar is Francis of Assisi. He is known to the world as a man who gave away all he had to the poor, and who was kind to birds and animals. What is less well known is that even before his death in 1226 thousands of people had sworn to follow his example and adopt a life of poverty and preaching. Francis himself was well aware that he was no organizer: other men ran the actual organization of the order of the Franciscan Friars, even during Francis' lifetime. Francis was not a priest (he did eventually become a deacon) and he would never accept a title higher than that of 'Brother Francis.' The word friar itself derives from the word 'frere' meaning 'brother'.

At the same time as Francis was working in Italy, a similar movement was becoming popular in Spain. This was led by St Dominic: like Francis he saw the need for an order dedicated to preaching and ministering to the poor. Dominic was especially concerned with preventing people falling into heretical beliefs. Unlike some of his contemporaries, he was sure that this could only be done though argument and by example, not with the use of force. He differed from Francis in some ways: he was a priest (in fact a black canon of the kind we have already discussed) and a very capable organizer. He laid slightly less stress than Francis did on the need for absolute poverty among the members of his Order. Whereas the Franciscans followed rules drawn up by St Francis himself, Dominic decided that his friars should adopt the rule of St Augustine, to which he added detailed 'Constitutions'.

The difference between the monk and the friar is well put by Augustus Jessopp - *'The monk was supposed never to leave his cloister. The Friar in St Francis' first intention had no cloister to leave. Even when he had where*

*18. St Francis of Assisi displays his stigmata (left),
the only surviving representation of St Francis on a Norfolk screen.
The other figure is St Leonard, in the dress of a medieval monk.
From the screen at Hempstead next Eccles parish church (NRO, PD 273/29)*

to lay his head, his life work was not to save his own soul but first and foremost to save the bodies and souls of others. The Monk had nothing to do with administering to others'.

The friars were really fulfilling needs that in an ideal world would have been satisfied by parish priests, so they were not direct rivals to the monks. Their enormous popularity showed that there were simply not enough priests of high quality to fill the needs of the ordinary people in towns throughout Europe. As Robert Grosseteste, Bishop of Lincoln, told Pope Gregory IX, the Franciscans in England *'illuminate our whole country with the bright light of their preaching and teaching. f your Holiness could see with what devotion and humility the people run to them to hear from them the Word of Life, to confess their sins, to be instructed in the rules of living, and what improvement the clergy and regulars have gained by imitating them, you would indeed say that 'upon them that dwell in the valley of the shadow of death hath the light shined'.*

It needs to be stressed that the friar's sources of income were intended to be very different from those of the monks. Whereas the monks lived off income from their estates, the friars were mendicants, that is they lived by begging. Even the friary buildings were not owned by them at first, but were held in trust. As St Francis wrote:

> *The friars should be delighted to follow the lowliness of poverty of our Lord Jesus Christ, remembering that of the whole world we must own nothing; but 'having food and sufficient clothing, with these let us be content' as St Paul says. They should be glad to live among social outcasts, among the poor and helpless, the sick and the lepers, and those who beg by the wayside.*

There were several other orders of friars, some of which failed to catch on. The two others that were successful were the Carmelites and the Augustinian friars. The beginnings of the order of the Carmelites are rather obscure but derived ultimately from a group of hermits living on Mount Carmel in Palestine. The Augustinian friars grew out of groups of hermits in North and Central Italy. Like the Augustinian canons we have already met they took their inspiration from instructions given in letters of St Augustine of Hippo. At first these groups formed their houses in out of the way places, but soon they began to establish town houses like the other mendicant orders.

The various orders of friars had other names too, some of which show up as street names in English towns, even when the friary buildings themselves have completely disappeared. Franciscans were also known as Friars Minor and, more commonly, as Grey Friars. Dominicans were known as Friars Preachers, and as Black Friars. The Carmelites were called White Friars: these names derive, of course, from the colour of the robes they wore. The Augustinian friars were not known by any colour but usually as Austin friars. This has sometimes been since corrupted to Ostend in street names as in Yarmouth where Ostend Row marks the site of the cell of the Austin friars in the town. (Part of a doorway can still be seen in the wall of the Society of Friends' meeting house, which now occupies the site.)

The first friars to come to England were the Dominicans: they arrived in 1221, establishing a house at Oxford that year and one in London in 1224. Their third house in the country was that at Norwich, founded in 1226 - a clear indication of Norwich's importance in the Middle Ages. This house was north of Colegate. In 1259 an agreement was reached between the Black Friars of Norwich and Dunwich deciding where the friars of each house could beg: Dunwich was allotted all of Suffolk plus Mendham and Rushford parishes while Norwich was to have all the rest of Norfolk. This must have become redundant fairly quickly as three other houses were soon established in Norfolk: at Yarmouth in about 1270, Lynn in 1272 and Thetford sometime between 1325 and 1345.

The Franciscans also arrived in Norwich in 1226 (coincidentally, this was the year that Francis himself died). Their house was on King Street, at the top of what is now Prince of Wales Road. They too followed up with houses at Yarmouth and Lynn. One of the Franciscan friars at Yarmouth lived up to popular images of Friar Tuck - John Rokeby weighed 24 stone. This fact was

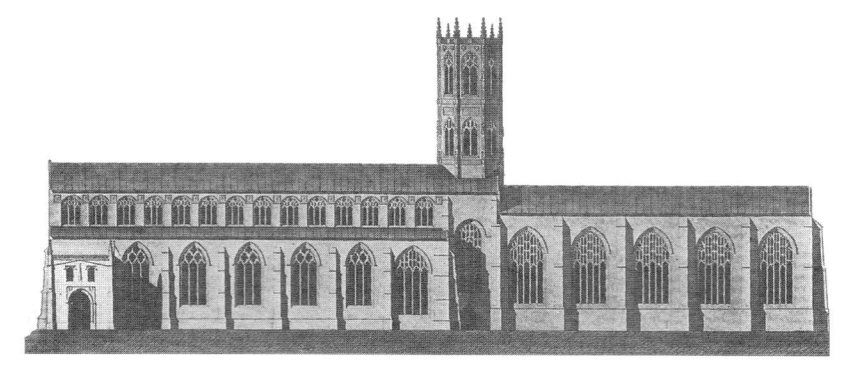

19. Reconstruction drawing of Norwich Dominican friary by Benjamin Sewell

The friars

thought important enough to be recorded on the 1492 Yarmouth borough court roll! In 1346 the Franciscans established a friary at Walsingham to minister to the many thousands of desperately poor pilgrims who visited the town. The priory there objected to this rival establishment but they failed to have it moved, unlike the monks at Bury St Edmunds who were successful in forcing a Franciscan friary to move outside 'their' town.

The other two orders of friars came in slightly later and seem to have been invited in by lay patrons rather than to have come as a deliberate decision of the central organisers as was the case with the first two orders. Burnham Norton was the first Carmelite friary in Norfolk, founded in 1241. This was only three years after the Saracens had captured the mother house on Mount Carmel. Knowles suggests that the Burnham house was founded by friars fleeing from this disaster: if so they must have found North Norfolk a great change after Palestine. The Carmelites came to Norwich in about 1256: their house was on Whitefriars, on the site now occupied by Jarrold's printing works. They set up houses at Lynn in 1269, Yarmouth in 1278, and Blakeney in about 1295. (Blakeney may seem a rather surprising place to establish a friary, but the towns of the North Norfolk coast were booming and important ports at this time.) The Carmelite friars of Norwich were in effect adopted by the Corporation in 1488: from this date they treated the Corporation as their founder although they had actually been founded by a Norwich citizen, Philip Cowgate.

The Austin Friars were welcomed into England by a royal letter of 1349. They established houses at

20. Yarmouth Franciscan friary: the west walk of the cloister

Norwich, founded shortly before 1289, Lynn, founded before 1293, and Yarmouth, founded before 1311. (The house at Yarmouth was actually in Gorleston, across the river from the main town. However the friars did have a cell in the town of Yarmouth itself.) They also had a house at Thetford. This was founded by John of Gaunt in 1389, an unusually late date for a friary foundation: it was in fact to be the last friary founded in England. The sites of these later houses were acquired by a mixture of gifts and purchases. The Austin house at Norwich, for example, was developed from a gift of land at St Michael Conesford to them by Bartholomew de Acre in 1289. Three years later they obtained the five neighbouring properties by purchase.

21. Arch from Norwich Carmelite friary reused at Arminghall Old Hall: the arch is now in Norwich Magistrates' Court (NRO, from MC 186/4)

The friars spread rapidly throughout Europe during the thirteenth and fourteenth centuries. By the end of the fourteenth century there were almost 200 friaries in England - 65 Franciscan, 58 Dominican, 39 Carmelite and 34 Austin. Whereas monks usually sang or read their services to and for themselves, the friars encouraged people to come to their churches, share in their worship and listen to their preaching. Because of this, their churches tend to be a rather different shape than monastic churches, as can well be seen at Norwich. The monastic church of Norwich Cathedral has a long, narrow nave, ideal for grand and impressive processions. The nave of the Blackfriars church (now St Andrew's Hall) is much broader, to allow people to come closer to the pulpit and hear the sermons. The friars made a special feature of the service called Compline, which was held, at the end of the working day: townsfolk were urged to attend this service in friary churches after their day's work was done.

The friars could come into conflict with parish clergy over three issues - the right to preach, to hear confessions and to bury the dead, all of which had potential financial implications of course. In 1300 Pope Boniface VIII issued

The friars

regulations that the friars might preach in their own churches and in certain public places, that only those friars licensed to do so by the local bishop could hear confessions, and that if anyone was buried in a friary cemetery, the friars would give a quarter of the profits to the person's parish priest.

The friars preached both in their own churches and also in the open air in small towns and villages. The Dominican friary in Norwich had an open-air pulpit in the yard outside the church, still an open space today. (Although monks are not thought of as preachers, some did like to preach of course: Abbot Samson of Bury St Edmunds, who was a Norfolk man, was noted for the strong local accent in which he gave his sermons.) Roger Twyford, a Norfolk Austin friar of the 1390s, is a good example of an itinerant preacher: Fuller's Worthies says that he was commonly called 'Good-luck' because he brought success to others, and in consequence was welcomed wherever he went.

The second speciality of friars was the hearing of confessions. The Lateran Council of 1215 expected people to make confession once a year. This was normally done in Lent, and by most people in Holy Week itself: this would have created considerable pressure of work on the local priest. People queuing up for confession can be seen in sculptures of the confession scene on many East Anglian 'seven sacrament' fonts. In many populous urban parishes the priest must have been glad to have friars to help in the arduous task of hearing all the confessions. Several of the Norfolk friars were especially eminent in this field. The Lynn friar Geoffrey of Salisbury was one of the most noted confessors in England: he would reduce the sinner to tears by his own copious weeping. When Alexander de Bassingbourne confessed to him he began light-heartedly, 'as though telling a tale'. Geoffrey began to weep for him and soon Alexander was in tears too, resolving to give up his sins and become a friar himself.

From the later fifteenth century, important people would employ a full time confessor to act in effect as their spiritual and moral director: friars were often chosen for this role. Walter of Diss was one of these: he was confessor to John, Duke of Lancaster, and his wife. Walter was a supporter of Pope Urban and preached against the Pope's opponents - those who fought against them were promised as many indulgences as if they were fighting the Moslems in the Holy Land! Another friar from Diss who became noted in this area of expertise was William of Diss, confessor to Henry V. The Franciscan friar John Brackley was chaplain to Sir John Fastolf: he is mentioned many times in the Paston Letters.

22. The tower of Lynn Franciscian friary

The friars

Living in the towns and depending (at least at first) entirely on begging, the friars were, of course, more 'in your face' that the monks. Like beggars today they were the object of strong opinions. The friars had supporters among both the poor and the rich. We naturally have less information about the poor but we do have the evidence of the Peasants' Revolt. Jack Straw, one of its leaders, confessed that they intended to kill all bishops, canons, monks and rectors of churches, but not friars. Indeed the embracing of poverty by the friars was thought by some people to have been one of the factors that led the peasants to rebel against their lords. There is no doubt that the earliest friars in England did embrace poverty in the spirit of St Francis - a visitation of the custody of Cambridge (which included Norwich) was made in 1237: it found that the friars had no cloaks.

The unpopularity of the friars in some quarters is revealed by a charter of Richard III ordering mayors, sheriffs and bailiffs to protect them. They were told to punish those who stirred up the people against the friars, encouraging them to burn their houses, tear their habits off their heads and beat them up. A local opponent of the friars was a woman called Margery Blackster who in 1428 told off one of the Yarmouth Carmelite friars for begging: she said that he would please God better by leaving the friary and going to the plough.

These different views continue to be held by historians. W R Richmond wrote of the friars at Yarmouth - *'they touched with love and pity the lives of thousands of the poor and sorrowful, who but for them would have died without knowledge of the Redeemer, or without being brightened by one ray of human sympathy'*. In contrast, Hudson and Tingey wrote of the Norwich friars *'as they were nominally mendicants and lived upon charity, it may be questioned whether they added much to the economic strength or progress of the city'*. (They do not consider what the friars may have added to its religious life).

It is clear, however, that many Norfolk people did appreciate the work of the friars: they showed their approval by leaving money to them in their wills. A few early wills survive among the Norwich archives that illustrate this. John Bond (in a will probably of 1248 but this date is not certain) left four shillings to the Friars Minors and two shillings to the Friars Preachers: his cape and a cup were to be sold to raise the money. In 1272 William de Dunwich left one mark each to three friaries - Minors, Preachers and Carmelites. He left 20 shillings to the Friars of the Sack. In contrast he left chalices rather than money to his 'favourite' monasteries - Horsham St Faith, Hickling, Mendham (in Suffolk), and St Benet's - perhaps this indicates that at this early date friars were not thought to be wanting such treasures.

Almost half the people leaving wills in Norwich between 1370 and the Dissolution left money to all four friaries and a good number asked to be buried in them. Some of the bequests were large ones. When William, Lord Morley, was buried in the Norwich Austin friary, his mortuary was his best black horse. He also gave the friary his 'principal complete vestment' with one cloth of gold embroidered with the heads of ladies. The same house was given 100 marks by Joan Fransham in 1422. Thomas Kerdiston left the Austin friars the enormous sum of 300 marks in 1446 as well as a silver cross and a pair of silver basins - naturally these were to have his name inscribed on them. The Austin friars did have to take on a perpetual commitment in return - they were to find three friars to celebrate for Kerdiston's soul and those of his two wives for ever. Anne, Lady Scrope, of Harling left the Austin friars in Thetford 'a vestment of silk or of cloth of gold' worth 40 shillings.

Evidence of the popularity of friars in Yarmouth can be seen in the 23 wills for the single year 1349 transcribed by Henry Swinden: two of the testators asked for a friary burial and no less than 15 left money to friaries. Here too there was an occasional precious gift: William de Motte bequeathed to the Yarmouth Carmelite Friars a silver cup with a pelican on the lid. We have come a long way from the simple poverty of St Francis and his first followers and from the rumour quoted in Paul Richards' History of Lynn that 'the Carmelites in South Lynn are said to sleep in their coffins'.

23. Brass to friar William Yarmouth, now at Halvergate parish church

The friars

In fact, like several of the orders of monks before them, the friars had rapidly become victims of their own success. As more and more people left them money and property in their wills, the original ideals of poverty inevitably fell away to a very great extent. As with the monks, occasional efforts were made to tighten things up. For example in 1357 the Prior General of the Austin friars issued new regulations for his order. He said that from now on only the sick could sleep on feather beds or wear linen: other friars who had acquired these luxuries had to sell them within fifteen days. No friar was ever to have in his possession more than two florins as 'pocket money'. Anyone who had more than that must give the extra into the common treasury. No friar was to own anything made of silver - some obviously did and again they had to sell these items within fifteen days and give the money into the common treasury.

As the friaries acquired wealth, their buildings also became grander. The church of Santa Maria *Scala Caeli* - literally Ladder of Heaven - outside Rome was a pilgrim church of international repute: it contained the altar at which St Bernard was praying when he saw the soul for whom he prayed leave Purgatory and ascend a Ladder into Heaven. In 1497 Nicholas Lathe of Norwich left money for a priest to go to Rome and say five masses for his soul there. However, from the early sixteenth century, people were leaving bequests for masses to be sung at the *Scala Caeli* in the church of the Austin friary in Norwich. This was a local copy of the one in Rome where, presumably, the same indulgences for the remission of sins were granted. A typical will is that of Isabel Norwich, quoted by Kirkpatrick. She asked for five masses at the Norwich *Scala Caeli*, and also for a *trental* or set of 30 masses for herself and for her friends at each of the other Norwich friaries (trentals are discussed later in this book). There were similar altars in the Austin friaries at Lynn and Thetford.

By the time that Thetford Austin friary was founded, it was automatic for a founder to give some estates to a friary. John of Gaunt gave the house 36 acres in Thetford and Barnham (in Suffolk), and within a year they were given land in six other Norfolk parishes. By the Dissolution all friaries owned land, although on a much smaller scale than most monasteries. Burnham Norton friary owned 68 acres of land in 1538 and Blakeney about the same: even the smaller monasteries could own many hundreds of acres of land.

Some groups of Franciscans did try to keep true to the ideals of St Francis and split away from the main order which they saw as betraying the principles of their founder: they were known as 'observants'. Although they spread through Europe they did not really catch on in England: their first house was not set up until 1482 and they only had six houses in this country altogether. No houses were founded in Norfolk.

Lay people - both men and women - who wanted to be part of a friary community might purchase a *letter of confraternity* from it. This granted them special participation in the services and prayers of the friars. Some women doing this referred to themselves as sisters of the friary in their wills, such as Joan Cook in 1478 and Margaret Est in 1484, both 'sisters' of the Norwich Grey Friars. Anne, Lady Scrope, describes herself as a sister of the Norwich Austin friars in her will of 1498.

The friars were traditionally regarded with suspicion by monks and canons and much of the criticism of them comes from these sources. Occasionally such disputes might reach the Bishop's courts and thus be entered in the records. In 1484, for example, the prior of the Benedictine priory in Great Yarmouth complained that the Grey Friars had illegally taken it upon themselves to bury three men who had been killed on board the King's ship, the *Elizabeth*. The prior travelled three times to the Bishop's court in Norwich while the case was being considered: presumably the principle involved justified the expense of 10s 5d. However, on a local level, there could be friendship and support between the various religious groupings. The monks of Norwich Cathedral priory would entertain the Grey Friars (or supply them with food) every Christmas. They might also employ them: in 1505 they paid a friar to serve the Cathedral priory church at Eaton.

As we have seen, the great era of enthusiasm for friars was between about 1220 and 1300. As well as the four orders of friars, which we have discussed, several other groups were formed, most of which faded out relatively quickly: in 1307 the Pope suppressed the groups which were thought to be too small to be viable. A small group called the Friars of the Sack had established two Norfolk houses, at Lynn and Norwich. Both were dissolved in 1307. The Black Friars of Norwich acquired the site of the Friars of the Sack: they promised to look after the last remaining friar there who was 'old, broken and blind'. Over the next twenty years they expanded the site by obtaining the neighbouring properties. The process is recorded in the City Court rolls but no sums of money are mentioned: again it seems likely that some properties were given to them but others purchased by them. They built a large new house, although a small part of the old house of the Friars of the Sack still survives (the crypt and Becket's Chapel). Most of the church built by the Black Friars in the early fourteenth century was itself destroyed in a disastrous fire of 1417: however the great east window facing Elm Hill

The friars

survived. The friars still had their Colegate site and they retreated there while a new and even grander church was built for them. St Dominic himself had written that no friary church should have walls more than thirty feet high, nor use vaulting (except in the choir), nor contain funeral monuments. These rules had clearly long been forgotten: the friars had so far departed from the original ideals of poverty that the clerestory was faced with stone and emblazoned with the arms of one of their benefactors, Sir Thomas de Erpingham. The church was taken over by the city at the Dissolution and was used for civic functions: it is the only complete friary church still in existence in England.

In contrast, the house of the Friars of the Sack at Lynn has disappeared so completely that even its site is not known. Another group, the Pied Friars, had a house beside St Peter Parmountergate churchyard in Norwich: this too was dissolved in 1307, their building being taken over by a college of priests. There was another small group of friars near St Julian's church in Norwich dedicated to the Blessed Virgin: the references to them are very obscure and it is not even clear if they were actually one group or two: they too would have disappeared in 1307. (Blomefield suggests that one group survived until it was wiped out during the Black Death, but this seems unlikely).

THE BUILDINGS

The buildings occupied by monks, canons, nuns and friars were all so similar that they can be discussed together. Monastic buildings can be considered under two headings: the church and the living quarters.

THE MONASTIC CHURCH

As we have said the whole point of a monastery was to offer up prayer, hence the church was much the most important building in the complex. The churches of all monastic orders followed very much the same pattern and can be considered as a whole here.

Almost all monastic churches - like almost every parish church in medieval England - were designed along an east-west axis, with the high altar at the east end and all the other altars along east-facing walls. This passion for the eastern altar is unique to England and the reason for it is not known. Because the east end, with the high altar, was the most important part of the building, work always started at this end, gradually working along the church towards the west. However ordinary people would enter a church at its west end so we shall begin our survey of the monastic church from this end.

The west front of the church might well be highly decorated, as can be seen above all at Castle Acre. Dickinson calls it 'one of the loveliest and most elaborate facades of any small English monastery'. Binham, although not so grand, is architecturally more important, perhaps the most advanced building of its day in England. The window of the west front has *bar tracery*, where the pattern is formed by intersecting moulded ribs of stone (all earlier windows use *plate tracery* where the shapes are cut through the solid stone). It used to be thought that the earliest example of bar tracery in England was at Westminster Abbey in the 1240s onwards. However the chronicler Matthew Paris tells us that the west front of Binham was built by the prior Richard de Parco. Parco was prior between 1226 and 1244, so if Paris is right the bar tracery at Binham is the earliest in England.

Norfolk monastic buildings were in fact often innovative both in style and in building materials. The vault of the undercroft of Norwich Dominican friary is of brick and one of the earliest examples of the use this material in the city. There is an even earlier example however within the fabric of Beeston priory where the extraordinarily large bricks used are still visible: this may well have been the first use of brick in Norfolk since the time of the Roman Empire.

The buildings

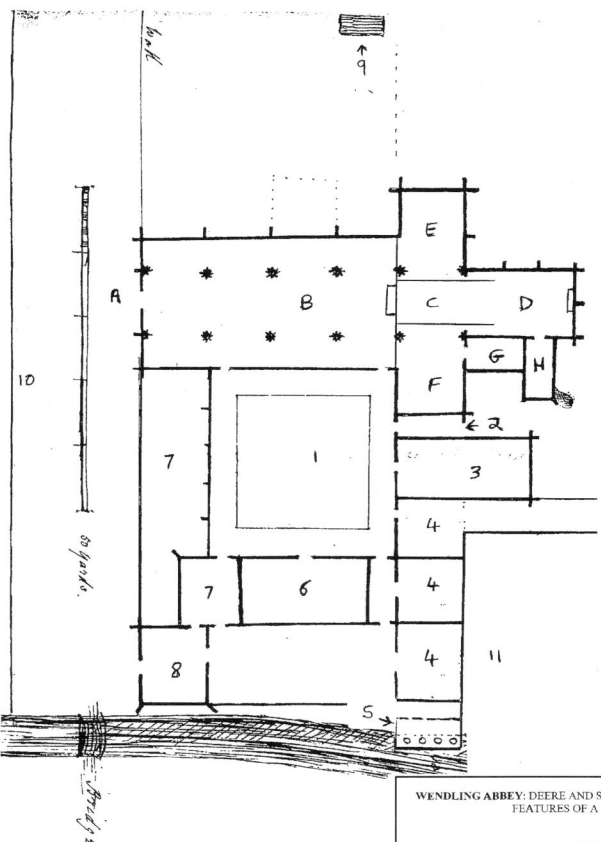

24. Wendling Abbey, marked to show typical features of a monastry. *(Based on drawing in NRO, MS 4580)*

WENDLING ABBEY: DEERE AND SPURDENS PLAN MARKED TO SHOW THE FEATURES OF A TYPICAL MONASTERY

THE CHURCH

A THE WEST FRONT
B THE NAVE, WITH ALTAR AT THE EAST END
C THE QUIRE, SEPARATED FROM THE NAVE BY THE PULPITUM
D THE PRESBYTERY, WITH HIGH ALTAR AT THE EAST END
E NORTH TRANSEPT, WITH ALTARS AGAINST THE EAST WALL
F SOUTH TRANSEPT, WITH ALTARS AGAINST THE EAST WALL
G CHAPEL
H SACRISTY

THE LIVING QUARTERS

1. THE CLOISTER, WITH DOORS INTO THE CHURCH AT THE EAST AND WEST ENDS
2. PASSAGE [OR *SLYPE*]: THIS MIGHT ALSO BE USED AS A PARLOUR
3. THE CHAPTER HOUSE
4. STORE ROOMS AND WARMING HOUSE BELOW, DORMITORY [OR *DORTER*] ABOVE
5. LATRINE–BLOCK [OR *REREDORTER*] BUILT OVER A STREAM
6. DINING ROOM [OR *FRATER* OR *REFECTORY*]
7. GUEST ROOMS AND ALMONRY
8. INFIRMARY
9. FISH PONDS
10. PRECINT WALL
11. MONKS' CEMETERY: THREE STONE COFFINS WERE FOUND HERE

The earliest uses of squared knapped flints were also monastic - the first known is that in Yarmouth Benedictine priory, followed by the fourteenth century east wall of the Chapter House at Thetford Cluniac priory.

25. Binham priory: Bucks' drawing, showing the west window. (NRO, MS 4579)

Another innovation was the development of flushwork, where the squared flints are set into stone to produce decorative patterns. The earliest known examples are monastic gatehouses - the friary at Burnham Norton and St Ethelbert's gate at Norwich Cathedral priory. Flushwork patterns can also be seen in the gatehouse at St Benet's and on the great arch at Walsingham priory.

Going into the church one would enter the long western arm, called the nave from the Latin word for boat. This presumably refers both to a resemblance to an upturned boat and, more importantly, to the church as the ark of salvation. The nave would be a relatively long, high and narrow space leading the eye towards the high altar at the east end, behind the rood screen surmounted with its loft with an enormous crucifixion scene above. To people in the Middle Ages, used to living in small clay lump or wattle and daub houses, a monastery must have been a dramatic and impressive building.

The longest nave, of course, was that of Norwich Cathedral, 12 bays long. (The nave as we see it today is actually 14 bays long, but the two eastern

The buildings 53

bays were in fact part of the monastic church: round piers with spiral grooves mark the division.) The naves of the smallest monastic houses might be three or four bays long. Even relatively small houses like Creake had aisles to the naves, with a *triforium* and *clerestory* above. It is this 'three-storey' effect of the church interior that characterises churches such as Binham and Norwich Cathedral priory. In both cases the naves still have their Romanesque austerity. At Wymondham, the nave and triforium at Wymondham are still those of William d'Albini. However the clerestory here, with the roof with its wooden angels, is a mid fifteenth century design. Some smaller religious houses could not afford the expense involved in such ambitious designs and might omit the triforium. Because of the cloister abutting one side of the church, the windows on side would obviously have to be high up. This can be clearly seen at Marham where the round windows are above the line of the cloister roof.

Some monastic churches did not have aisles to the nave - even the church of a high status monastery like St Benet's did not, (the reconstruction drawing made in the eighteenth century by Anthony Norris is wrong to give it a south aisle). The nave of the much smaller church at Beeston was only three bays long, also with no aisles. However it did have transepts, and further chapels were built later so there were plenty of altars for the canons to pray at - the house was only founded for four canons. Friary churches always had aisles to the nave but not usually to the chancel.

26. Interior of Binham priory

The larger churches would take many years to build, often starting from small beginnings. When the Earl of Warenne founded Castle Acre he gave the monks the services of one of his serfs, Ulmar, who was a stone mason. The church was begun in 1090 but not formally consecrated until about 1147. The Cathedral priory took about the same length of time to build. Work started here in 1096. When the founder, Herbert, died in 1121 the east end and the first two bays of the nave had been completed. Herbert's successor, Everard, managed to finish the church and the main monastic buildings before his retirement in 1145. Both these great churches had taken about half a century to complete. Because of the lack of good building stone in Norfolk it had to be imported. As is well known, much of the stone used to build Norwich Cathedral was brought in from Caen in Normandy. Other stone came from Barnack in Northamptonshire. Recent work by Roberta Gilchrist has revealed a third source: the quarries at Quarr in the Isle of Wight. The stone would have been brought in ships to Yarmouth, off-loaded there and carried up the river and along the canal that ran up to what is now the Lower Close.

One should think of the nave of a medieval church as a parish hall rather than a church as we know it. There were no seats of course, only stone benches along the walls for the infirm (hence the saying 'the weakest go to the wall'). There would have been people standing about, talking and transacting all kinds of business. The most dramatic use of the nave would have been as a processional space: on feast days the monks would process through the nave chanting and swinging censers. Norwich Cathedral priory even had a gigantic statue of an angel that on special occasions was let down through a hole in the roof (which can still be seen) to fill the nave with incense. The angel was used for the first time in 1401, the first year of a seven-year papal indulgence granted to people visiting the Cathedral, which (as intended) brought a great influx of pilgrims. It was used twice a year, at Trinity and at Corpus Christi. However when Henry VII was at the Cathedral at Easter 1487 the angel was used especially in the king's honour.

Monastic churches, like parish churches, were much more highly decorated than today - there would have been wall-paintings of saints and biblical scenes and gilded and painted statues. This would be the case even in friary churches. Kirkpatrick tells us that the choir of the Black Friars church in Norwich was adorned with wainscot painted and gilded with Biblical scenes and legends. This must have been 'rescued' at the Dissolution as in his time (about 1713) it was in a private house in St Andrew's parish. He could make out some of the inscriptions on it including the names of three medieval mayors of the city - Richard Brown, Edmund Sedgeford and William Norwich - who were benefactors of the friary. There is a unique example of the wall-painting of a friary church still visible at the Franciscan friary in Great Yarmouth.

At least one Norfolk monastery shared the East Anglian tendency to build round towers: there was one at St Benet's. Some monasteries had more than one tower (as did St Benet's which also had a western tower).

The buildings 55

27. Norwich Cathedral priory: tower and spire
(NRO, ACCN Clark 18/10/91)

Norwich Cathedral priory had a separate clocher or bell tower to the west of the main church: this has totally disappeared. The Cathedral priory was perhaps the only Norfolk monastic church to indulge in the luxury of a spire: the present one is fifteenth century and although it appears to be made of stone is really a wooden spire with a very thin stone cladding on its surface.

As we have said, there would be a wooden screen at the east end of the nave, as in any other medieval church. These are the screens that can still be seen in many Norfolk churches, usually with paintings of saints. Part of the screen at Binham can still be seen (though out of position): some of the medieval images can still be made out in spite of having been since painted over with black-letter text. Above the screen was a rood loft (the only partial survival in any Norfolk church is the one at Attleborough). On special occasions the priest would go up the stairs and perform part of the service from this loft, standing at the feet of the Crucified Jesus that dominated the church. The modern rood and crucifix at Wymondham give an impression of what a medieval church might have been like.

Behind the high altar in a monastic church was a stone screen called a pulpitum (there was usually a pulpit attached to it for preaching purposes). The pulpitum separated the lay part of the church from the monastic part. It can still be seen at Norwich Cathedral priory and also at Binham, where it now forms part of the east wall of the parish church. Part of the stone screen at Ingham forming the pulpitum also survives. The division between the lay and the monastic part of the church might sometimes be merely a wooden screen as at Beeston.

Beyond the pulpitum was the *choir*, or part of the church where the monks worshipped for so much of the day. This contained two rows of wooden stalls, often finely carved, facing each other: the arrangement can best be seenat Norwich Cathedral but also at Ingham and in Blakeney parish church. The stalls each had a misericord or tip-up seat with a carved bracket underneath: this was for the monk to rest against during the lengthy services. They are often finely carved, with both sacred and secular images. The religious significance may well be lost to us as we are not familiar with the stories and legends of the time. For example, a picture of an elephant was obviously fun to carve but it had a message as well. It was believed that an elephant had no joints in its legs and so could never lie down. The only way it could sleep was by leaning against a tree. This means cutting the tree down could capture it. Just like Adam, the elephant could fall because of a tree!

Most monastic churches were cross-shaped with a central tower. The two short arms of the transept were used for altars. This was especially important

The buildings

28. Ingham: the remains of the stone pulpitium, with monks' stalls beyond

in English churches where, as we have seen, all the altars had to be against east walls. Those monks who were priests (and by the later Middle Ages almost all were) would use these altars for the many daily masses that they said. The nunneries at Thetford and Carrow were also cross-shaped, an indication of their relatively high status. The church and chapter-house at Thetford were rebuilt in 1160-1176 when the nuns replaced the monks.

The importance of the eastern part of the church can be illustrated from the example of Creake. In the early fourteenth century a large chapel was built to the north east of the church which is still a dramatic ruin. There was a disastrous fire in 1484 when the church and buildings burnt down. The abbey appealed for help to the king as their patron: he gave them £46. 13s. 4d. Private citizens also responded to the crisis. In 1495 Sir William Calthorpe left Creake abbey £74. 6s. to build the choir and presbytery and in 1504 Walter Aslak left money for the aisle north of the choir. It seems that the eastern part of the church was thus rebuilt after the fire while the nave was more or less abandoned by the end of the century and it is the eastern end that is by far the more complete today.

It was fashionable in England in the eleventh and twelfth centuries to have a round east end to a church, ending in an apse. This can still be seen at

Norwich, where there is an ambulatory or walk-space all around the choir. The great churches at Binham, Castle Acre, Wymondham and Thetford all had round east ends. In the last three of these churches, however, the later fashion for a square east end (as popularised by the Cistercians, for example) has meant that the east end has been rebuilt or extended to provide a square end. With an increasing devotion to Our Lady there would often be a Lady Chapel built on, either added to the east end (as at Norwich, since demolished) or to the north of it (as at Thetford and Castle Acre). Cistercian churches were all dedicated to the Blessed Virgin Mary anyway so had no need for a separate Lady Chapel.

Although we have spoken of the east end of the church as the monastic part, it does not mean that lay people never went there. At Norwich, for example, the chapel where St William's shrine stood was at the north-east end of the church so the pilgrims would be admitted to see this. In some houses important local laymen might join the monks in the choir for certain services. Several monastic churches were actually parish churches as well, with the nave acting as the people's church. This was the case at Binham, Wymondham and Weybourne (and, perhaps, at Blakeney). At Ingham the relatively late priory was tacked onto the already existing parish church. These arrangements were not always happy ones.

Disputes at Wymondham led the parishioners to build their own tower at the west end of their part of the church in the mid fifteenth century. Part of Wymondham church was intended for the monks, the rest for the parishioners. In 1249 it was agreed that the town should have the nave, north aisle and north-west tower. The priory was to have the chancel, south aisle and south-west tower. At the end of the fourteenth century the monks at Wymondham had moved their bells from the lantern tower (which had become unsafe) and put them in the north-west tower, although this tower had been given to the parishioners. They pulled down the lantern tower and put up the present octagonal one a bay further west. They then built a solid wall across the western end of this tower. This was allegedly to make the tower stronger but in fact totally separated the parishioners' church from the monks' church. The monks then brought back their bells to the central tower, walling up the north-west tower to prevent the parishioners putting their own bells there.

Matters came to a head in 1410 when the parishioners hung three bells in the north-west tower to disturb the monks and also imprisoned the prior for two days after Epiphany to prevent him saying Mass on that important feast day. The parishioners were eventually allowed to have their bells in the tower provided they did not ring them during the monks' rest times, between 6 pm

29. Wymondham priory church: the part between the two towers has been maintained as the parish church of the town (NRO, MC 640/22/4/1)

and 6 am. They then produced a petition signed by 3,000 local people saying the tower was so low they could not hear their own bells. In the mid fifteenth century they finally built the grand tower which still stands at the west end of the church. After this the monks and people appear to have lived together in peace. At the Dissolution the parishioners asked the king if they could buy the lantern tower and south aisle (including the monks' dormitory above it). The king agreed and also gave them timber, stone and glass from the Chapter House to use for rebuilding the south aisle. The result of the parish buying the lantern tower has been to produce Wymondham's well known spectacle of a church with a large tower at each end.

The arrangement seems to have worked better at Binham where there is no record of any disagreement. In 1432 the monks at Binham granted to the parishioners the right to have services in the church 'as often as they please as is usual in other parish churches in the deanery of Walsingham'. They were allowed to have a bell of 800 pounds weight provided they did not ring it to the prejudice of the office of the priest of the priory. There is a medieval 'seven sacrament' font at Binham - a purely monastic church would, of course, have no need of a font.

There do not seem to have been any disputes over church-sharing at Weybourne but the history of this building is a more complicated one. The church at Weybourne before the canons came consisted of a nave with a tower at its east end (this tower can still be seen, standing to its full height on the south face). The canons built their chancel to the east of this tower. In the late thirteenth century a new nave was built south of the old one (which became its north aisle). The canons much enlarged their part of the church in the early fourteenth century, adding chapels and transepts. They appear to have been over-ambitious as the north transept aisle was abandoned: the blocked-up arches on the north side of the choir can still be seen. The parishioners at the same time extended their nave further west and added a western tower.

The monastic parts of all three of these churches fell out of use after the Dissolution. They are all now ruinous. At Weybourne, as at Wymondham the two towers both survive, in part at least. However at Weybourne, because of the nave being shifted south, the two towers are not in line so that the effect is less dramatic.

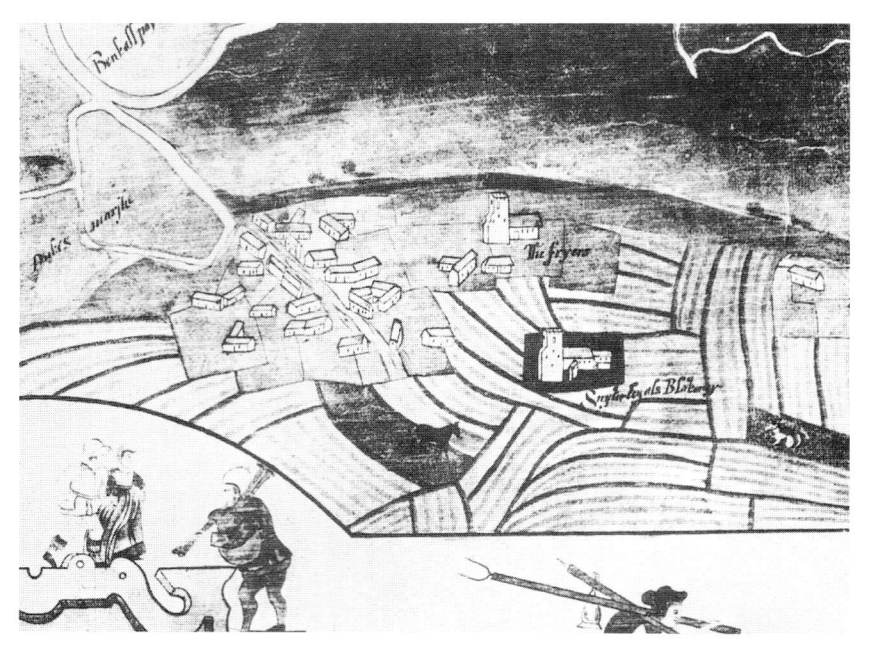

30. Map of Blakeney in 1586, showing the friary church and parish church (NRO, MC 106/28/1)

The buildings

At Blakeney the Carmelite friars are thought by some people to have used the chancel of the parish church as their own church. The main piece of evidence centres around John Calthorpe. In his will of 1503 Calthorpe asks for his 'sinfull body' to be buried in the chancel of the church of the White Friars. In fact his brass can be seen even today - just in front of the rood screen in Blakeney parish church. Another piece of evidence is the medieval doorway in the north wall of the chancel, looking towards the friary buildings. On the other hand the chancel of the parish church seems too small to have been the centre of worship for all the friars attending the provincial chapter held here seven times between 1389 and 1533.

Even more convincing is the evidence of the first known map of Blakeney, drawn in 1586, which clearly shows two churches - the friary church is on the far side of the monastic buildings to the parish church. It would seen that Blomefield was right when he suggested that Calthorpe's brass was originally in the friary church but was moved into the parish church after the Dissolution. However, even if the chancel was not monastic it probably conveys the feel of a monastic church more than any other in Norfolk with its (modern) rood screen and stalls with fine misericords.

The parish churches that the Cathedral monks served from their cells at Lynn, Aldeby and Yarmouth are all well worth visiting in their own right, although that at Yarmouth was very badly damaged by bombing in the Second World War. St Margaret's at Lynn contains spectacular brasses to two mayors of the borough, Adam de Walsoken, who died in 1349 and Robert Braunche, who died in 1364. The church at Aldeby is much smaller, but still on a grand scale for a village church, being built with north and south transepts (the latter has since disappeared). These are all monastic churches in the sense that they were served by monks, who did not have their own churches. This is clearly the case at Aldeby and also at Lynn where the foundations of the monastic Chapter House adjoin the south wall of the parish church. The position at Yarmouth is less clear - Pevsner and Wilson imply that the monks did have their own church. However a 1753 map of Yarmouth shows the priory cloister immediately south of St Nicholas' church so there was almost certainly no separate church here either.

Friary churches were originally much plainer in design than monastic churches. However, as the friars became richer, this distinction disappeared to a large extent - the one surviving friary church, that of the Dominicans at Norwich, for example, could hardly be called a simple building. Nevertheless it is much less rich in decoration than a large parish church of the same date, for example St Peter Mancroft in Norwich. It also illustrates two characteristics for friary churches. It is a wide building to allow more people to hear the preaching which was such an important feature of the friars' life. The other characteristic is the walkway between nave and chancel surmounted by a central tower. At Norwich Dominican friary the tower has fallen down but the walkway still survives between what are now the Blackfriars Hall and St Andrews Hall. In contrast, at the Franciscan friary at Lynn the central tower is the only part of the building to survive.

THE LIVING QUARTERS

The living quarters of a monastic house follow much the same pattern, whether the house was a monastery, a friary or a nunnery. The principal buildings were grouped around the cloister; a square green surrounded by a covered walkway. One side of the cloister was the nave of the church: this was normally on the north side of the cloister so that the tall church did not block out the light and heat of the sun. However considerations of drainage were paramount and in some monasteries the cloister is on the north side of the church as at Norwich Dominican friary. It seems to have been relatively common for canons to have their cloisters on the north side of the church - examples still visible include Weybourne and Thetford St Sepulchre. At Ingham too the cloister was north of the church: the arches of the cloister walk adjoining the church can still be seen.

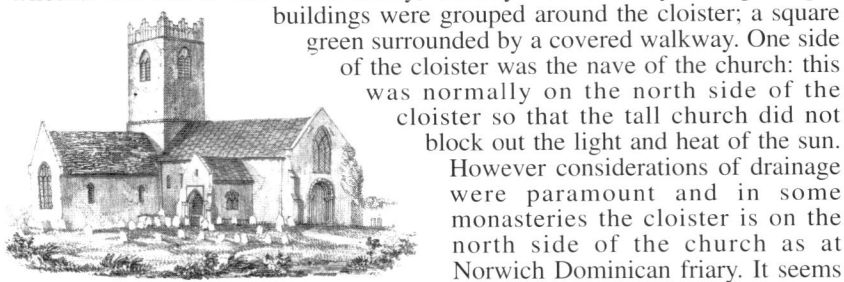

31 Aldeby church: as a monastic cell of the cathedral priory, this was a superior buiding for a village church, with north and south transepts (NRO, MS 4576)

The covered walk of the cloister linked the major monastic buildings, which opened off it. It was also where the monks did their work, copying and illuminating manuscripts. The book cupboards where they were stored can still be seen in Norwich Cathedral cloister. The cloister wall would be plastered and decorated: in 1713 two large painted crucifixes were still visible in the north west corner of the cloister at Norwich Black Friars.

The best surviving cloister in Norfolk is that of Norwich Cathedral priory. We are doubly fortunate in having both the building itself and the account rolls that give details of the building work. Gifts and bequests paid for much of it. According to William Worcester, Master Henry of Wells left 210 marks (£140) for vaulting the bays of the north walk of the cloisters. Geoffrey Symond left £100 for the cloisters in 1410: his executors appear to have paid up in instalments of about £18 a year. Some of the money went on the two western bays of the south walk. John Wallington was paid 2s. 4d. a week for 33 weeks in 1415 and 1416: he was carving the bosses of the vault there. The main series are of scenes from the Book of Revelation. Lesser bosses

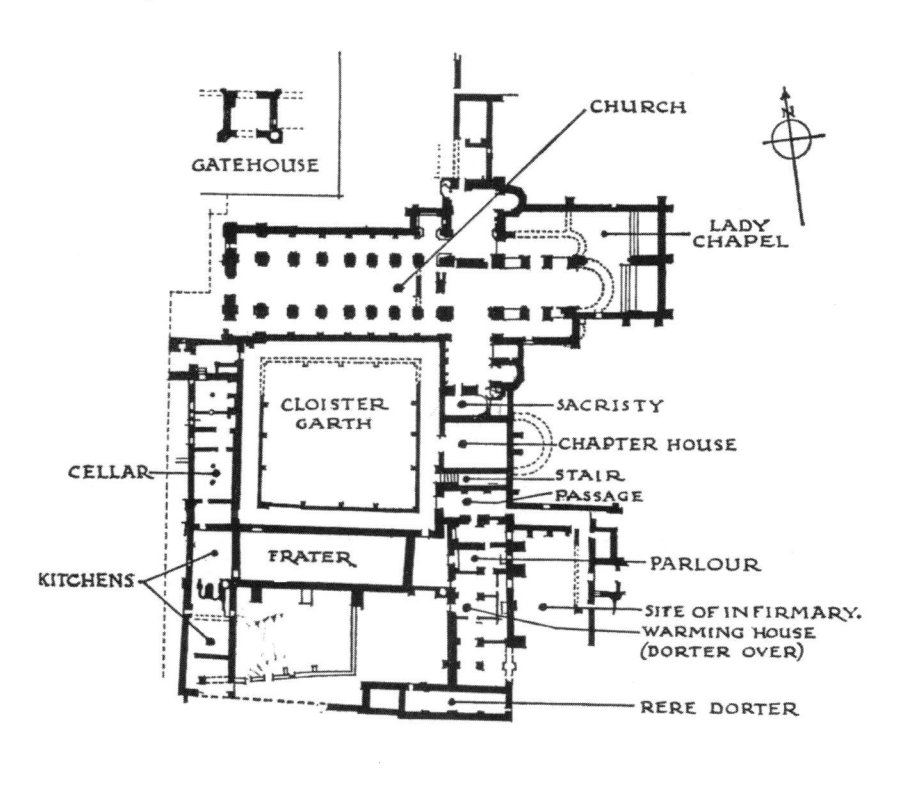

The buildings

32. Monastic plan: Thetford St Mary priory

in the same bays include a dragon and a 'green man': these were carved by a Dutchman called Brice. This is one of the few cases where we can look at a feature in a Norfolk monastery and know the name of the artist and how much he was paid for his work.

Friary cloisters tended not to be built alongside the church but to be separated from it by a small courtyard, as at Norwich and Thetford Dominican friaries and at Walsingham. The courtyard was needed to provide light for the windows of the church, which would otherwise be blocked by the two-storey cloister buildings. Another characteristic of friary buildings can also still be

33. Monastic plan: Norwich Dominican friary

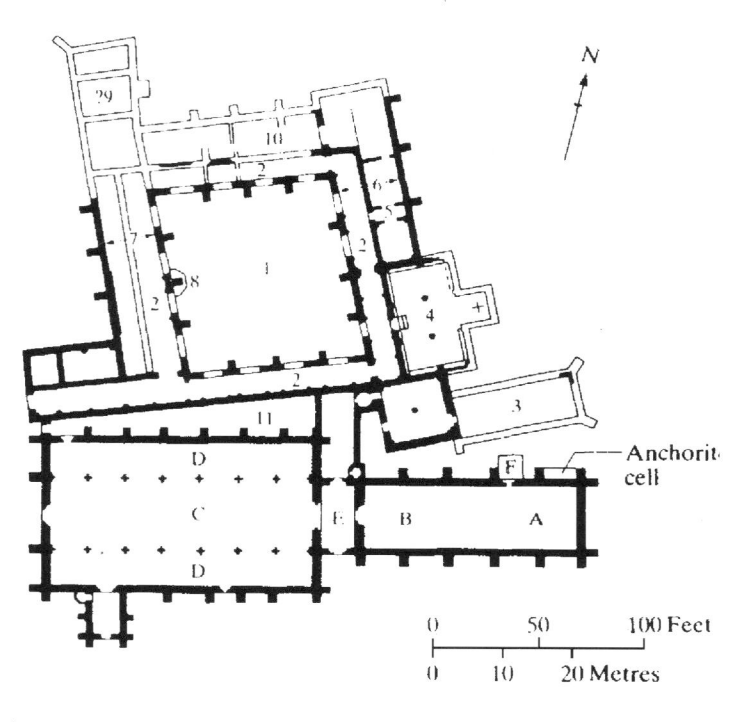

1	Cloister garth	7	Refectory	A	Presbytery
2	Cloister alley	8	Pulpit	B	Choir
3	Books	9	Kitchen	C	Nave
4	Chapter house	10	Cellar or store	D	Aisle
5	Passage	11	Lane	E	Walking place
6	Dormitory			F	Vestry or sacristy

seen at Norwich Dominican friary: they tended to build on top of the covered walkway of the cloister, whereas in other monasteries the buildings were usually erected behind the cloister walk rather than over it.

We can walk around a typical cloister describing the buildings. The church normally occupied the whole of the north side, usually with a door into it at each end of the cloister. The west wall of the south transept took up the first part of the east walk of the cloister. This was often separated from the rest of the buildings by a slype or passage allowing access to the eastern parts of the monastic site. This might be expanded into a parlour where talking between monks would be allowed during the lengthy time of day that silence was the rule elsewhere in the monastery.

The remainder of the east range of the cloister would be of two storeys, the dormitory above running along the whole range, the Chapter House and other rooms below. If there was no slype, the Chapter House might abut directly onto the south transept of the church, or there might be a treasury or a sacristy between the two.

The Chapter House was the central building in the monastery after the church itself and the one on which most money was spent. The monks met there every day to confess to the prior or abbot, to hear reading from the Rule of the house and to discuss monastic business. It normally had seats ranged along two or three of the walls and remnants of these can sometimes still be seen. Because the dormitory was above, the height of the Chapter House was obviously restricted: this might be overcome by having a kind of ante-room actually under the dormitory leading to the Chapter House beyond, which could then be a much higher building. Most Chapter Houses were rectangular, either with a straight east wall as at Binham, or with an apse as at Castle Acre and at Thetford St Mary. Other variations were possible: the Chapter House at Norwich Dominican friary was only two bays long but three bays wide while that at Lynn Benedictine priory was hexagonal. As it was a high status building, recognisable parts of the Chapter House may still survive, such as the arch at Wymondham and the side walls at Bromholme. The entrance bays to the Chapter House at Norwich Cathedral priory survive although the actual building has long disappeared.

The remaining part of the lower floor of the east range would have a variety of uses. There would be storerooms there and the rest of the space might be used as a

34. Wymondham chapter house arch

warming room, the only room in the monastery apart from the kitchen where a fire was permitted. The fireplace of the warming house at Binham can still be seen: the adjacent window seats must have been very comfortable resting-places during a cold day in a Norfolk winter.

At first all the monks slept in the dormitory, but the practice very early developed of the head of the house having his own accommodation. This might be next to the dormitory or elsewhere in the monastery, often on the west side of the cloister as at Castle Acre. In the later Middle Ages the custom developed of partitioning the common dormitory into what were in effect single bedrooms. These might be used for study as well. At the Gorleston Austin Friary a friar who wanted to raise money to travel to the Holy Land was permitted to 'sell' his chamber to another brother. There would need to be stairs up from the cloister to the dormitory of course: - there is a fine example at Castle Acre. Often the dormitory often had another set of stairs at the north end opening directly into the transept of church and known as the 'night-stair'.

The dormitory would extend beyond the cloister southwards ending in the *reredorter* or toilet-block, which would be built over a stream: streams were often deliberately diverted for this purpose. Remnants of these arrangements can still be seen at Thetford and above all at Castle Acre. Although it now appears that the stream under the latrine block at Castle Acre runs straight down to the kitchen, in fact the unclean water was carefully separated from the pure. Monks had a high standard of cleanliness and hygiene. The standards within a monastery were undoubtedly superior to those of any lay house, even those of a royal palace. Francis of Assisi wrote praised 'Sister Water' in his famous *Canticle of the Sun*: he wrote that she was 'useful, humble, precious and poor'. Many friary water supplies were better than those of the surrounding towns - after the Dissolution both Lincoln and Gloucester took over the water supply system of the Franciscan friaries in their towns and used them for the citizens. Lynn Austin friary ran a conduit from a spring on the Bishop's estate in Gaywood to their friary in the centre of town in 1383. The large stone-lined drains of monastic houses have often been supposed by later generations to be underground passages built for nefarious purposes!

Most monastic houses had a *lavatorium* or washing-place with running water in the cloister, usually next to the entrance of the dining room. This arrangement can still be seen at Binham. Another washing-place survives at Norwich Cathedral priory, where however it is in the south west corner of the cloister.

The buildings

The *south* range of the cloister was taken up with the communal dining-room (also called the *frater* or *refectory*). This might be on the ground floor or on the first floor with storage rooms below. The building was usually long-side on, but the Cistercians had a habit of setting theirs at right angles to the cloister. The kitchen was often next door, but might be moved further away out of the main cloister range: this was probably a precaution against fire spreading and burning down the whole monastery. (Fire was a continual danger. In 1286 the church and monastic buildings at Westacre were destroyed by fire.

We have already mentioned the serious fire at Creake. Two of the Yarmouth friaries burnt down in the early sixteenth century.) The kitchen would also need water supply of course. That at Castle Acre was originally in the corner of the cloister but was later moved further south and actually built over the stream.

All monks ate their meal in silence while one of the community read from the Bible: the pulpit and the stairs leading to it occasionally still survive. Walsingham priory is one place where this arrangement can still be clearly seen: this dining-room also has a beautiful east window. The dining-room walls would be painted: the Last Supper would be the most appropriate scene. One splendid series of refectory wall-paintings survives at Horsham St Faith: the main image is of the Crucifixion, with nine scenes (of which seven survive) relating to the story of the foundation of the house, as told earlier in this book.

35. Norwich Cathedral priory: the monks' dining room

The range of buildings along the west side of the cloister was normally also two storied, with storage space on the ground floor. The upper floor was usually for guests although the exact use varied. The guest-house of Norwich Cathedral priory and the prior's quarters (and those of his guests) at Castle Acre are both along the west range.

As the abbots and priors became more separate from the remaining monks, they would increasingly have their own set of rooms. Examples are the fine set of prior's rooms in the west walk of Castle Acre and the detached range at Thetford St Mary. The large fourteenth century hall at Yarmouth Benedictine priory was probably the prior's hall, rather than the monastic dining-room as previously thought. It is now part of the Priory School. The oak panelled ceiling dates from the early sixteenth century and one of the fireplaces bears the arms of the last prior, William Castleton. Panels of the arms of England and France that were originally in this Hall are now on the porch of the nearby parish church. Many of these buildings were rebuilt in a more luxurious style in the early years of the sixteenth century, such as the lodging of the prioress at Carrow and the prior's house at Norwich Cathedral.

36. Thetford St Mary: the monks' dining room

They made very acceptable residences for Tudor gentry after the Dissolution, which is why they have survived. The last prior at Norwich Cathedral, William Castleton continued to live in the same house in his new role as the first dean: the dean still lives there today.

Almost all monasteries had an infirmary, usually to the east or the south east of the main cloister. The essential parts were the Hall (where the sick stayed), the chapel and the kitchen. The Hall was at first one large room, but later tended to be split into cubicles. The infirmary building might itself be set round a small square or cloister as at Thetford St Mary. Friaries did not usually have a separate infirmary, again probably because of lack of space on their cramped urban sites.

The buildings

More functional buildings would be further out in the monastic precinct, often in a range or grouped into an outer court, like the buildings at Castle Acre or in the Upper and Lower Closes of Norwich Cathedral priory. They would include a granary for storing grain, a mill for grinding it into flour, a bakehouse and brewhouse. There would be buildings of a kind to be found on the estates of any lord, whether monastic or lay, - stables, a smithy, a dairy, hen houses, animal sheds, beehives. At Norwich the granary, bakehouse and brewery were grouped around the Lower Close. The almoner, with the almonry hall, almoner's granary and his own house, took up the southern end of the Upper Close. There were separate houses for other monastic officials - the communar and cellarer - along the east side of Almary Green. There would also be fishponds, orchards and gardens. The very large pond just to the north of Beeston priory church is probably one of the original fish ponds of the priory and earthworks for ponds can be seen at Carbrooke, St Benet's and other Norfolk monasteries.

37. Norwich cathedral priory: the guest quarters

The gardens at Norwich Cathedral priory have been analysed for the Norfolk Record Society by Claire Noble, using the evidence of the gardener's account rolls. There were several different gardens within the precinct. The kitchen garden was where vegetables such as garlic, leeks and beans were grown. These were used to make a pottage or thick soup, which was

38. Thetford St Mary: the prior's lodging

39. Beeston priory: the north transept, with the pond to the north of the church (NRO, MC 530/8)

eaten for supper. There were orchards with apples, peas, cherries, walnuts and hazelnuts. The infirmary had its own garden growing herbs and fruit. He also grew a good deal of saffron, which was thought to be effective against plague. The cellarer's garden had formal alleys or walkways so it was perhaps in effect a pleasure garden. The hostilar had a garden too, presumably for the noble guests to relax in. Friary sites tended to be much smaller than monastic ones but they too might have space for gardens. According to C. J. Palmer, the Franciscan friary at Great Yarmouth had a 'strawberry yard' and mulberry trees: at least one of the trees was still standing in 1571, over 30 years after the friary had been dissolved. When ten-year-old Nicholas Hyndry went to Gorleston friary in about 1500 it was to gather crocus flowers (years later he was to claim that the friars held him there against his will and forced him to take their vows).

1. St. Augustine writing on a scroll. From the pulpit in Burnham Norton parish church. (NRO, MC 640/4/8)

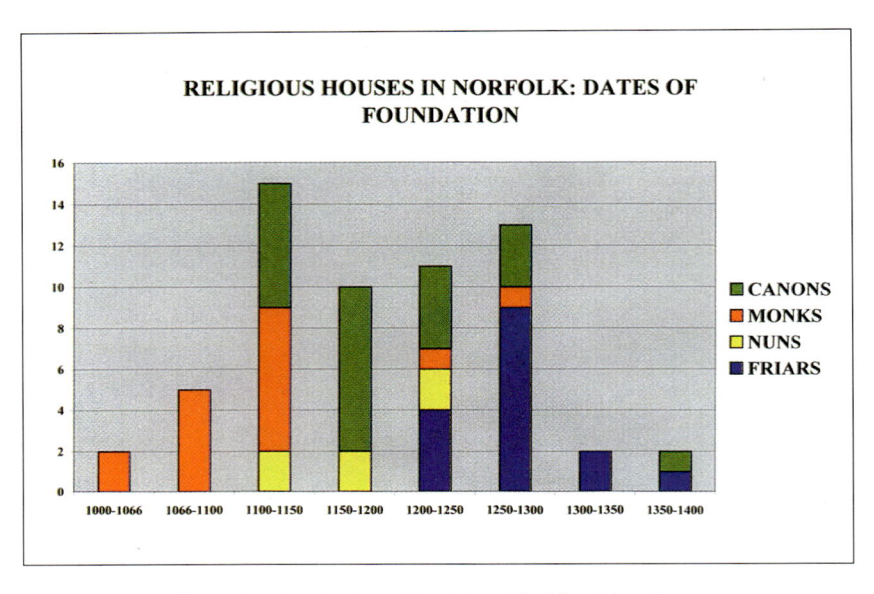

2. Graph to show the dates of foundation of Norfolk religious houses.

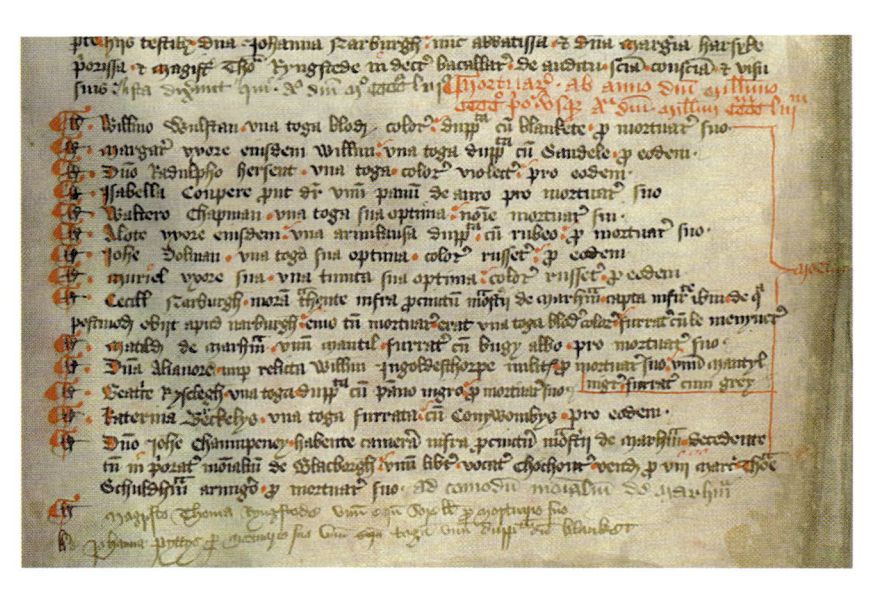

3. List of people and the mortuaries they gave in return for burial in the cemetery of Marham abbey. (NRO, Hare 1)

In purificatione beate marie — **februarius**

Benedic ✠ domine iesu xpe hanc creaturā cere supplicantibus nobis. ⁊ infunde ei per virtutē sancte crucis benedictōnem celestem: vt qui eam ad repellendas tenebras humano vsui tribuisti. talem signaculo sancte crucis tue fortitudinem ⁊ benedictionem accipiat. vt quibuscunq̄ locis accensa siue apposita fuerit. discedat diabolus ⁊ contremiscat ⁊ fugiat pallidus cum omnibus ministris suis de habitationibus illis. nec presumat amplius inquietare.

seruientes tibi. Qui cū deo patre et spiritu sancto viuis et regnas deus.

Per omnia secula seculorum. Amen. Et dicuntur omnes orationes cū Oremus. sub eodem tono. Non dr̄ Dn̄s vobiscū. nisi ante priuatā orationē tātū. Or̄o.

Domine sancte pater omnipotēs eterne deus. q̄ oīa ex nichilo creasti. et iussu tuo per opera apum hunc liquorem ad perfectionē cereorȝ peruenire fecisti. ⁊ qui hodierna die petitionem iusti symeōis implesti. te humiliter precamur: vt has candelas ad vsus hominū. ⁊ sanitatē corporȝ ⁊ animarū pre paratas. siue in terra siue in aquis. p inuocationem sancti nois tui. ⁊ per intercessionē sancte marie semper virginis. cuius hodie festa deuote celebrantur. ⁊ per preces omniū sanctorum tuorȝ bene ✠ dicere et sancti ✠ ficare digneris vt huius plebis tue. que illas honorifice in manibus portare desiderat. teq̄ laudando exultare. exaudias voces de celo sancto tuo. ⁊ de sede maiestatis tue

culorȝ. Amen. Oremus. Oratio.

Omn̄ps sempiterne deus. q̄ hodierna die vnigenitū tuū vlnis sancti symeonis in templo sancto tuo suscipiendū presentari voluisti: tuā supplices depcamur clementiā. vt hos cereos. quos nos famuli tui in tui nois magnificentia suscipiētes gestare cupimus. luce ac celos bene ✠ dicere ⁊ scti ✠ ficare. atq̄ lumine supne benedictiōis accedere digneris. quatin⁹ eos tibi dn̄o deo nr̄o offerēdo dignā. ⁊ scto igne dulcissime tue claritatis succēsi. in templo scto glorie tue

representari mereamur. Per eūdē dominū nostrū iesum xp̄m filium tuū qui tecū viuit et regnat in vnitate eius dē spirit⁹ sācti deus. Per omnia secula seculorum. Amē. Dominus vobiscū. Et cū spiritu tuo. Sursū corda. Habem⁹ ad dominū. Gr̄as agam⁹ domino deo nostro. Dignū ⁊ iustū est.

---

4. Early printed service book from Langley abbey; unusually this is printed onto parchment rather than paper. (NRO, NRS 19869)

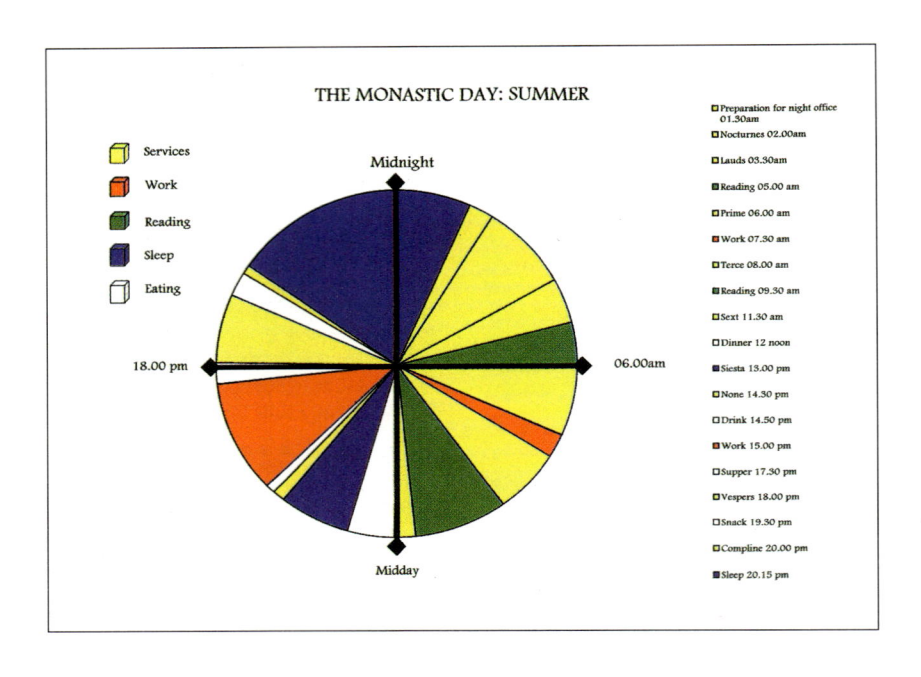

THE MONASTIC DAY: SUMMER

- Services
- Work
- Reading
- Sleep
- Eating

- Preparation for night office 01.30am
- Nocturnes 02.00am
- Lauds 03.30am
- Reading 05.00 am
- Prime 06.00 am
- Work 07.30 am
- Terce 08.00 am
- Reading 09.30 am
- Sext 11.30 am
- Dinner 12 noon
- Siesta 13.00 pm
- None 14.30 pm
- Drink 14.50 pm
- Work 15.00 pm
- Supper 17.30 pm
- Vespers 18.00 pm
- Snack 19.30 pm
- Compline 20.00 pm
- Sleep 20.15 pm

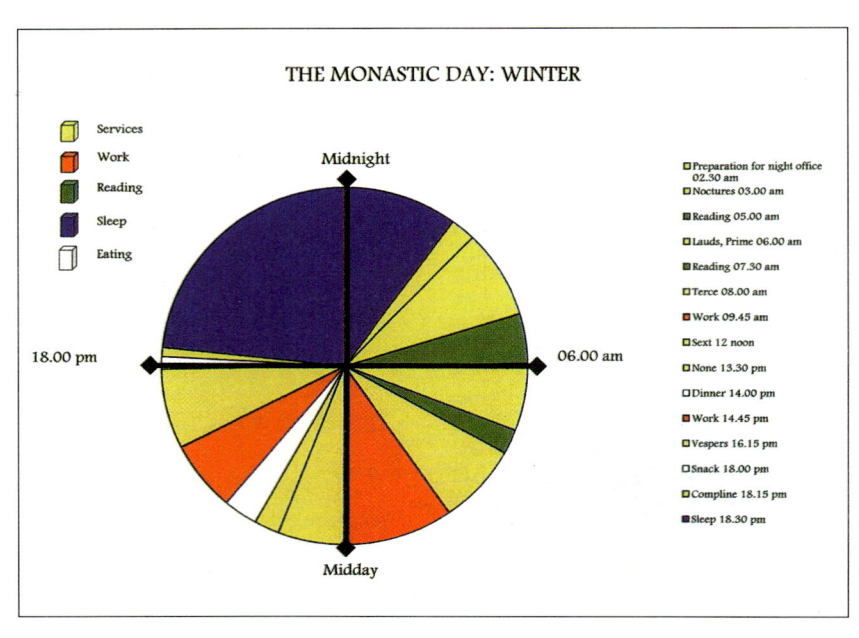

THE MONASTIC DAY: WINTER

- Services
- Work
- Reading
- Sleep
- Eating

- Preparation for night office 02.30 am
- Nocturnes 03.00 am
- Reading 05.00 am
- Lauds, Prime 06.00 am
- Reading 07.30 am
- Terce 08.00 am
- Work 09.45 am
- Sext 12 noon
- None 13.30 pm
- Dinner 14.00 pm
- Work 14.45 pm
- Vespers 16.15 pm
- Snack 18.00 pm
- Compline 18.15 pm
- Sleep 18.30 pm

7. Portrait of Robrt Catton, the prior of Norwich Cathedral, surrounded by his monks and holding a charter, 1524. (NRO, NCR 9g)

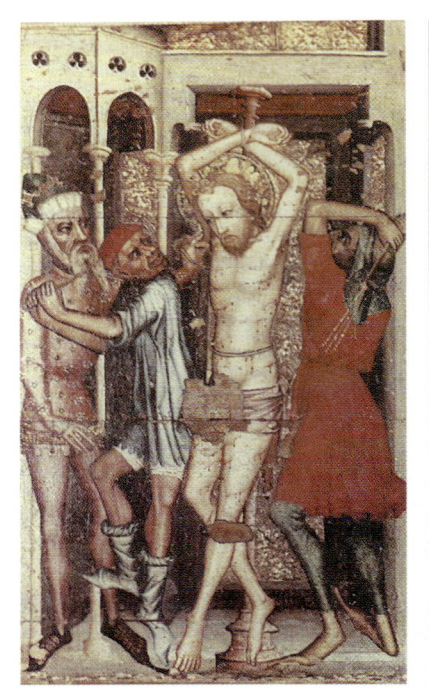

8 & 9. *Two scenes from the retable in Norwich Cathedral priory, probably a gift from Bishop Henry Despenser.*
(NRO, DCN 125/3)

10. *Bromholme: the gatehouse with a pilgrims' guest-house in the distance.*

11. *Burnham Norton friary: the gate-house*

12. The isolation of a Norfolk monastic house: Langley abbey.

13. Drawing by John Adey Repton of Norwich Cathedral priory cloister. (NRO, COL 8/11/2)

14. *St. Benedict (left), with another Benedictine saint. From the pulpit at Horsham St. Faith parish church.*

15. Marham abbey rent roll. (NRO, Hare 2213)

16. Castle Acre: the latrine block or reredorter.

The buildings

The monastic precincts would be surrounded by a high wall for security reasons. Access would only be possible through the gatehouse. These were often solid and imposing buildings and may be the best surviving part of the monastic house as at Pentney, St Benet's or Burnham friary. The gates would be closed at night and whenever danger threatened. According to Blomefield, Old Buckenham had a full-time lay janitor 'constantly attending at the monastery gates'. There were several gatekeepers at Norwich Cathedral priory: the office of head porter was held for life. When Nicholas de Clenchwarton was appointed in 1381, he was to receive a monk's loaf and a gallon of ale every day and the same food as the monks in the infirmary were being given.

Figure carving is preserved on the face of two monastic houses in Norfolk. The Ethelbert Gate at Norwich Cathedral has carvings (much restored) of a man with a sword fighting a monster, perhaps intended to represent the triumph of God's World over the world outside the monastic gates. The sculpture on the west front of the gatehouse at St Benet's has been protected from the weather by the windmill built over it in the 1720s. It features a man with a spear opposing a beast, which has a long forked tail, presumably intended to convey a similar message. Inside the same gatehouse, three faces still gaze down on the visitor, their mouths gaping. The most spectacular gatehouse in Norfolk is that at Pentney. This has side-rooms, some with fireplaces: these rooms were probably used as guest apartments. Two other fine gatehouses are at Thetford St Mary (often missed as it is set well away from the church and cloister) and at Castle Acre, with its beautiful combination of flint and brick.

40. Pentney: the gatehouse

41. Castle Acre gatehouse, before its restoration by English Heritage (NRO, MC 530/8)

Perhaps the friars, being more open to public access, did not need such imposing gatehouses. That at Burnham Norton friary is just an arched passageway with a small room over it: this room is described as a chapel in a Papal Indulgence of 1392. However their gatehouses could be substantial buildings too - Howard House in King Street, Norwich, appears to have been developed from the gatehouse of the Austin friary that formerly occupied the site.

The precinct walls of Blakeney friary are especially imposing as they are almost on top of the cliff. (However the brickwork in the gateway is a nineteenth century embellishment). The thickness of the walls of Norwich Greyfriars can be appreciated by following the surviving wall along St Faith's Lane. St Benet's abbey obtained a licence to fortify its precinct in the mid fourteenth century - the west gate and perimeter wall are presumably of this date. They were needed in 1381 when rebellious peasants twice besieged the abbey. On 20 June they frightened the abbot into giving up his court rolls which were burned outside the gate. They tried to attack the abbey again three days later but again failed to get into the precincts. Carrow priory was also besieged in 1381: it too was forced to surrender its manor court rolls, which were publicly burnt in Norwich. Presumably their peasants saw both these houses as oppressive landlords.

There are several other cases of attempts to break into monasteries by force of arms, so the walls and gates were very necessary. In 1212 Binham was besieged by Robert Fitzwalter after the prior (a friend of Robert's) had been removed from office. The monks were forced to eat bran and drink water from the drainpipes until Robert's men were driven off by the king's army. In 1307 a group of 25 men forcibly entered Horsham and remained at its gates for four months. Six years later a mob broke into Thetford Cluniac friary. Some of the monks fled into the church for sanctuary but they were pursued and murdered in front of the high altar. One man was later accused of murdering the prior's nephew in this incident but the jury found him not guilty. Norwich Cathedral priory was besieged several times by angry citizens objecting to its power within the city.

There were of course many small variations in the designs of individual houses. Binham, Norwich Cathedral priory and other houses had a parlour in the west range of the cloister, where the monks could discuss business with their lay servants and officials. The parlour at Norwich is now, (September 2001), the cathedral shop. The rooms next to it were for the use of the priors of Lynn and Yarmouth when business brought them to the mother house. At Norwich Dominican friary the guest range was on the side of the cloister opposite the church and the dining-room in the west range. A few small monasteries might not have a complete cloister. Peterstone appears to have been a simple 'L' shaped building with the church in the short arm and the

The buildings 73

living quarters in the long arm, with the refectory on the ground floor and the dormitory above it. At Langley an aisle was added on to the church taking up part of the cloister green which was thus no longer square in shape. At Beeston the prior had a separate house to the south of the cloister - where the farmhouse now is. The west front of the church at Burnham Norton still stands just a few yards behind the gatehouse: the site must have been a very cramped one at least originally. Humps and bumps in the ground mark out the rest of the church.

Walsingham friary, very unusually, had two cloisters. The second - or 'little' - cloister was fifty feet square and was south of the main cloister, with the dining-room between them. The west range was probably the kitchen but the functions of the south and east ranges are not known. The east range of the little cloister was rebuilt in quite a grand style in the early sixteenth century and is one of the best-preserved parts of the friary.

The monasteries had many buildings beyond their precincts, including granges and barns on their estates. Other buildings were at least in part for leisure activities. The prior of Norwich had a house downstream at Whitlingham: the ruins still can be seen off Whitlingham Lane. The prior would reach it by from the Cathedral water gate at Pull's Ferry: royal guests are supposed on occasion to have made this pleasant river journey too.

42. Walsingham Franciscan friary (NRO, MS 4579)

HOW THEY LIVED - DAILY LIFE

The routine of a monastery saw very few changes day after day. Christopher Brooke (*The Monastic World*) calls the monks routine 'a life of dedication and monotony beyond our dreams'.

Although religious services took up most of their day, the details of what they said and sung is rather a technical one and will not be discussed here in very great detail. Each order and each house might have slightly different routines: they would have especial celebrations of the feast-days of saints of their order for example. Some of the services would be sung and others spoken. The plainsong, or Gregorian chant, used at these monasteries can still be heard today in countries like Spain and Italy where the monastic tradition has continued unbroken: it remains one of the most moving forms of song known to humanity. The seven daily offices of St Benedict's rule derived from Psalm 119.164 - 'seven times daily have I praised you'. An eighth - *nocturnes* - was added by him and was to be said at two in the morning. In about 970 the REGULARIS CONCORDIA adapted Benedict's rule for English use. A typical day for a monk would be this:

2 am	Rise
2.30 am	*Nocturnes*
	Reading
Daybreak	*Matins* or *Lauds (said at daybreak and so called because the word 'laudete' (praise ye) occurs many times in Psalms 148 to 150 which were said at this service*
Full daylight	*Prime - said at the beginning of the day, i.e, sunrise*
	Private prayer
8 am	Wash
	Terce - originally at the 3rd hour of the day (9 a.m.)
	Mass
9 am	Chapter house
	Work in the cloister
12 noon	*High Mass - originally called sext - at the 6th hour of the day (noon)*
2 pm	Dinner
3 pm	*None - at the 9th hour of the day (3 p.m.)*
	Work in the cloister
6.30 pm	*Vespers - at the evening of the day*
	Drink
	Compline - from the word for 'completion'
8 pm	Bed

How they lived - daily life

This was a summer timetable (summer lasted from Easter to the middle or end of September in a monastic house.) The winter timetable allowed for the fewer hours of daylight. In the fourteenth and fifteenth centuries there were changes in routine in many (but not all) monasteries, designed to make the life less hard. The first service of the day took place at midnight after which the monks returned to bed. They rose again at about 7 a.m. The drinks break was expanded to a supper every day, except in Lent and Advent.

The daily offices were largely made up of psalms, short prayers (collects) versicles and responses (set prayers and intercessions, each with its own set reply). Adding prayers and litanies gradually lengthened services. Cluniacs tended to have the longest services of all. Cistercians and Austin canons had rather shorter services so they could undertake their work, whether labouring for the early Cistercians (who had special arrangements for the busy times of haymaking and harvest) or parish and hospital work for the canons. From the twelfth century onwards monks began to say private prayers, with just a server to assist and with no public congregation. From this time almost all monks were ordained, as were all canons and friars.

Within the yearly routine of services there were two cycles of celebration. One was built around commemoration of the key events in Christ's earthly life - Advent, Christmas, Lent, Easter, and Whitsunday. Nine feasts of the church were days of especial celebration: Christmas; Epiphany (6 January); Easter; Ascension; Pentecost; Trinity Sunday; Assumption Of Our Lady (15 August); Nativity Of Our Lady (8 September); All Saints (1 November). At these feasts, and at others deemed special by the monastic house, such as the anniversary of the date of its dedication, more ceremony was required. The community would wear copes at High Mass and at Matins twelve lessons would be read, instead of the usual three in winter and one in summer. On Palm Sunday the church would be decorated and then, as on the feast days, there would be a procession. The monks at Norwich Cathedral priory processed through the nave and cloister every Sunday. Their procession on feast days was longer involving leaving the church by the north transept door and going all around the outside of the east end of the church. This included walking through the monk's cemetery, no doubt a deliberate reminder of inevitable mortality.

The other cycle was that of the commemoration of saints. The important saints would be celebrated for a whole *octave* (the day itself and the week that followed). Lesser saints had a single day's celebration. Each order would stress the commemoration of its own saints and there would be local variations as to exactly which saints were celebrated. The most important days would be written in the service books in red ink rather than black - hence the phrase 'red letter day' for a day on which something important occurs.

A monastic *custumal* for Norwich Cathedral priory survives at Corpus Christi College, Cambridge. It dates from the fifteenth century and combines the Divine Office as laid down by St Benedict with many later additions. These show the influence of Fecamp, the monastery where Herbert de Losinga came from, and which itself was influenced by the customs of Cluny. The custumal shows that several saints not generally mentioned in English calendars were celebrated in Norwich. They included St William of course, but also St Felix, St Ethelbert and St Botolph.

As well as the formal services there were of course masses for the dead who had requested these and left money in their wills for the purpose. The most commonly used of these was a *trental* or set of 30 masses said on 30 successive days. (Richer patrons could pay to have them said in a shorter time to avoid having to spend a full month in purgatory.) Another variant was to spread the trental over a year, three masses on each of the 10 major feast days (the nine mentioned earlier and Candlemas). This was known as a *Gregorian trental* and the practice had a rather gruesome origin. According to legend, Pope Gregory's mother had had an illegitimate child while young, whom she had murdered and buried. The Pope, not knowing this, naturally thought his mother had gone to heaven when she died. However one day, while at Mass, he had a vision of her as a demon exuding flame from every orifice. She then told him to say the masses in the right order over the following year. He did this: she appeared to him once more but now she was radiant - the masses had done the trick.

A typical example of such a bequest to a Norfolk monastery is that of John Arlingham of Topcroft who died in 1437. He ordered the canons at Mountjoy to celebrate a trental of St Gregory with *placebo* and *dirige* for his soul: these are parts of the service for the dead whose names are derived from their first words (in Latin of course). Arlingham gave a further 2s.6d. for a requiem mass. In 1502 Philip Curson asked for a St Gregory's trental at Norwich Black Friars. The priest saying it was to have 10 shillings a year: this was to continue for 20 years. Although a Norwich alderman, Curson lived at Letheringsett and chose to be buried there. His rural background is shown in that he left 12 ewes, a ram and the lambs they produced to sustain the priest or friar saying his trental in the Black Friars!

How they lived - daily life 77

In some houses there were so many masses to be said that priests might actually be hired by the monks or friars to say the masses for them. These were not so highly-valued. John Kerdiston, in his will of 1466, insisted that the masses he ordered at Norwich Austin friary were to be celebrated by the friars themselves and not by hired priests. The high regard for friars saying funeral masses is reflected in the will of John Wodehouse, Chancellor of the Duchy of Lancaster. The masses were to be in Norwich Cathedral but were to be said not by the monks but the friars of the four Norwich friaries, the Carmelites on the first day and the other three orders on the three following days.

Who were the people who chose the religious life? They were more numerous than we might expect - a rough estimate would be that one male in a hundred chose this calling. Because becoming a monk was a deliberate step in the direction of anonymity, and also because so few working records of monasteries have survived, even the names of most monks are unknown. The main exception in Norfolk is that of Norwich Cathedral priory where the account rolls survive. Dr Joan Greatrex has drawn out all the names of the monks at the priory from these records. As might be expected their 'surnames' show most of them to be from local towns or villages, with 'de Norwich', 'de Lynn' and 'de Yarmouth' occurring most frequently.

The only monks of whom much is known are those whose lives were in some way exceptional - saints, cardinals and bishops, chroniclers. Two Norfolk monks show up in the calendars of saints - and both of them did in fact travel. They are Walter of Cowick and Godric of Finchale. Walter was born in Norwich but became a monk at the Benedictine monastery at Bec in Normandy. He spent most of his religious life at Cowick, a dependent house of Bec just outside Exeter. He lived a life of extreme austerity, apparently based on fear: he had had a vision of 'Purgatory and all its Horrors' as a result of which he put on a hairshirt which he wore for the rest of his life. An atmosphere of sanctity developed around his relics but he seems never to have formally been declared a saint.

Godric is a rather more attractive figure. He was born in Walpole, Norfolk, and combined his trade as a merchant with many pilgrimages, visiting Jerusalem, Compostella and Rome. In about 1105 he sold all his possessions and became a hermit on an island off Northumbria. Later he moved to Finchale near Durham. He was about 40 when he settled there and he was to remain for over 40 years. He too wore a hairshirt and lived in austerity, but unlike Walter his gentler side is recorded as well. He would wander the fields in the snows of a Durham winter and warm frozen field mice and rabbits under his arms or by the fire in his hut. He was an early anti-hunt protestor as well. Once a hunted stag burst into his hut, shortly followed by the Bishop's huntsmen. On being asked where the stag was, Godric replied simply *'God knows where it is'*. Impressed by his holy appearance the huntsmen retreated apologetically.

Some Norfolk monks rose to the heights of their profession becoming bishops. These were usually monks at Norwich Cathedral priory. We have seen that several priors rose to become bishop in the early years of the Cathedral priory. The monks tried again in 1406 but the king refused to accept their choice, Alexander de Tottington. Alexander was imprisoned for a time at Windsor, but eventually the king relented and he did become bishop of Norwich in 1407. Some became bishops of other dioceses. In 1336 the monks of Norwich Cathedral priory elected one of their brethren to be Bishop but the Pope had another candidate in mind and would not allow the election: the unsuccessful monk, Thomas de Hemenhale, was compensated by being made Bishop of Worcester instead. Another monk from Norwich, Ralph de Warham, became Bishop of Chichester in 1218. Thomas Brinton, born about 1320, was a monk at Norwich Cathedral priory who was educated at both Cambridge and Oxford. He attended the papal court and became Bishop of Rochester in 1373. Knowles calls him a 'decent, sober and sturdy monk-bishop'.

The cathedral priory monk who rose highest of all was Adam Easton. He became a doctor of theology and left Norwich to attend the court of Rome, where he was appointed a cardinal. Easton died in 1397. His tomb can still be seen in the church of St Cecilia in Trastevere in Rome. He is described on it simply as 'Adam Anglo' - as he was the only English cardinal at the time this was sufficient identification. The tomb is decorated with the three lions of England, looking remarkably like domestic cats.

Friars became bishops too. This goes against the famous account by Thomas de Celano of the meeting in Rome of Francis and Dominic with the Bishop of Ostia, later to become Pope Gregory IX. The Bishop suggested to them that many of their followers might become bishops: both men said their followers were content in the humble roles that God had given them - Dominic himself three times refused offers of a bishopric. However, within a relatively short time, friars were accepting bishoprics. A few of these friars had Norfolk connections. Thomas de Colby, for example, was a white friar at Norwich who was famed for his knowledge of many languages: he was appointed Bishop of Waterford and Lismore in 1399.

One of the most interesting men to study at the Norwich Franciscan friary was Peter of Candia. His career illustrates how religion could offer opportunities of travel and of a rise to power and influence of a child born in poverty. Peter was a Greek, born in Crete of humble parents who died soon after he was born. He was brought up by a Franciscan friar and joined the Order himself, firstly at Padua and then in Norwich. He took a degree at Oxford and taught throughout Europe - in Franciscan houses in Russia, Bohemia and Poland, and at universities in France and Italy. In 1402 he became Archbishop of Milan. This was a time when there were two rival Popes - Gregory XII at Lucca and Benedict XIII at Portovenere. In 1409 the church met at Pisa in council to sort out the schism in the papacy: they finally deposed both Gregory and Benedict. They went on to elect a new Pope and chose Peter: he took the name Alexander V. Unfortunately the other two refused to resign so there were now three Popes! The countries Alexander had studied or taught in supported him but other countries did not recognise him as Pope. He died suddenly at Bologna the following year, so suddenly indeed that it was rumoured that he was poisoned: however there is no real evidence for this. His interest in English affairs is shown in his formal condemnation of the teachings of John Wycliffe. Alexander's tomb can still be seen in the north aisle of the church of San Francisco in Bologna.

Although heads of houses tended to come from the upper strata of society, this was not always the case - Daniel, abbot of St Benet's from 1140, had been a glassmaker by profession and had had a wife and child before his entry into the religious life. William, prior of Castle Acre in the fourteenth century, had no problem with his social status - he was the brother of the Earl of Surrey - but had to overcome a different stigma: he was illegitimate. This meant that at every stage of his career he had to obtain a special dispensation from his Bishop or the Pope before taking up any office. Permission was given for him to become prior but he must have resigned or been demoted later as in 1349 he and another monk were said to have spurned the habit and become vagabonds - perhaps they were fleeing from the Black Death?

WORK - BOOKS AND LIBRARIES

Apart from *prayer,* the other principal element of monastic life was work. Originally this meant physical work but, by the twelfth century, it meant copying and illuminating old texts and writing new books. The Benedictines explicitly declared this to be the only type of work suitable for monks. Although the Cistercians at first encouraged a return to physical work following the original Benedictine ideal, even they soon found it more convenient to use hired servants instead.

43. A monk reading, a misericord in Norwich Cathedral priory (NRO, MC 186/82)

The books would mainly be religious texts, sermons, service books for the church itself, but also works of philosophy such as the Greek classics. St Benedict himself recommended the pages of scripture, the teachings of the elders and the writings of the fathers of the church. The core of the latter would be the works of the 'four doctors' of the Latin church - Jerome, Augustine, Ambrose and Gregory. Later generations of monastic copyists would take on a wider range of texts of all kinds including grammar, rhetoric and the Latin classics. These books were manuscripts of course, copied in the cloister from the original: a monk might devote a whole lifetime to a single volume. Monastic copyists are undoubtedly responsible for the survival of many Latin and Greek works of history and philosophy which would have been lost had it not been for their endeavours.

Equipment needed for this work would include a desk, ink, parchments, pens, penknives, awls to give guidance to monks in ruling lines, reading-frames to hold the book being copied, rulers and weights. More important work was decorated: gold, red and blue were the main colours used. As Knowles says 'It may be fairly claimed that in the late thirteenth century the art of illustration reached levels of vivacity and imaginative beauty which it was never to reach again in England'.

Naturally, some monks were keener than others on study. In 1402 a monk was given permission to move to Thetford Cluniac priory 'because divine offices are there by day and night solemnly performed, and because the priory possessed a copy of divers books in which he desires to study'. One prior of

Wymondham was driven mad by studying too hard. His fate was a sad one: he was taken to Binham priory where he was kept in chains in solitary confinement until his death.

At first the Cistercians - with their stress on the simple life - had fewer books than the other orders. They were originally forbidden to use colours in the manuscripts they copied but, as we have seen, the ideals of poverty of the first generations of Cistercians soon lapsed. The Norfolk Record Office has a manorial rent roll drawn up by the Cistercian nuns of Marham in the fourteenth century, which has incredibly rich illumination for what is fundamentally a working document rather than a religious book.

Most of the literary works of art compiled in monasteries were destroyed at the Dissolution but some fine East Anglian examples have survived. It is not usually known in which monastery they were written but there is a distinctive local style of art, and some books have peculiar features tying them to an individual church. Some beautiful examples of local illuminated manuscripts are: -

The Bromholme Psalter, now in the Bodleian Library, Oxford. The calendar of Holy Days includes the feast of dedication of Bromholme priory, so this was presumably made by the Bromholme monks for their own use. It also includes many references to Cluniac saints (Bromholme was a Cluniac house of course).

The Gorleston Psalter, now in the British Library, London. This includes a reference to the dedication of the Gorleston parish church so it was presumably commissioned by the parish priest or a wealthy parishioner. We do not know where it was made - perhaps in Gorleston friary itself but it is impossible to be certain.

The Ormesby Psalter, also now in the Bodleian Library, Oxford. This appears to have been begun for a lay patron, but completed for a monk at Norwich Cathedral, Robert of Ormesby, who gave it to the Cathedral library. The calendar celebrates those saints known to be especially celebrated in Norwich Cathedral priory including St William. It has beautiful illustrations. N. J. Morgan says of it: *'the Ormesby Psalter artist has fortunately combined something of Gothic elegance with [the] qualities of solidity of form learnt from Italian painting'*.

As well as religious books, *chronicles* were also written in monastic houses and these are one of the prime sources for our knowledge of medieval history.

One such chronicler was Bartholomew Cotton, a monk at Norwich Cathedral priory. Another was John Capgrave of the Austin friary at Lynn. He was an important figure in his world. He acted as host to Henry VI when he visited the friary in 1446 and in 1450 went to Rome for the jubilee celebration of the Holy Year. He became Prior Provincial (head of the order) of England in 1453. He wrote many books including a *Chronicle* and a *Life of St Norbert*. The latter was in English verse and Capgrave presented it to John Wiggenhall, abbot the house of the white canons at West Dereham in 1440. He also wrote a verse life of St Gilbert in English. This was specifically intended for those Gilbertine nuns at Shouldham who could not understand Latin, an interesting insight into the ways in which nuns could be helped by their more educated male religious - nuns, of course, could not have the benefits of a university education. After his trip to Rome, he wrote *A Solace of Pilgrims,* in effect an early guidebook for other travellers.

Cardinal Easton, while living in Rome, decided to send all his books to Norwich Cathedral priory: presumably he planned to retire to his former monastery and take up a life of study in his old age. The books were packed into six barrels and took ten years to reach Norwich. By this time Easton was dead, so the books became in effect a bequest. They must have helped to replace the books lost in the 1272 riots, but were themselves dispersed at the Dissolution. Only five volumes of Easton's bequest are known to exist today - three in Cambridge, one in Oxford and one in Avignon. (There are a further five volumes which *may* be from his library.) However over a hundred volumes from the monastic library as a whole survive, again mostly now in Cambridge.

Friaries were especially noted for their libraries, again in sharp contrast to the ideals of St Francis. The original Franciscan community in Assisi had only one book - a New Testament - and even that was given away by Francis when a poor woman came begging and there was nothing else in the house to give her. However the friars soon came to realise that they needed good libraries if they were to fulfill their aspirations as preachers. The library in Gorleston friary was especially notable: it was given a large number of books by Henry Stanton, founder of St Michael's College in Cambridge (now part of Trinity College) in 1320. A new library was erected at the friary in 1429 and many more books were received at about this time: they were catalogued by the prior John Brome. The Norwich Austin friary also contained a well-known library. In 1458 Margaret Wetherby (widow of Thomas Wetherby, an alderman who had caused much trouble in Norwich in the 1440s) left the friary 100 marks for building a new library. She insisted that her name and that of her late husband were to be inserted in the window glass and on every desk.

Several Norfolk friars achieved academic or literary fame. These included Prior Tylney of Yarmouth Carmelite friary who was Professor of Divinity at Cambridge University in the mid fifteenth century and Robert Bale, who was the author of *Chronicle of the Carmelite Order*, and who left his library to Burnham Norton friary on his death in 1503.

Most of the libraries were dispersed at the Dissolution. Hook lamented - *'works of great value were sold, for next to nothing, to grocers and soap sellers. Whole shiploads were transported to the Continent, to become the possessions of wiser foreigners. Bale knew of two noble libraries, the contents of which were sold for the paltry sum of forty shillings to a merchant who used them as wastepaper: and who in ten years only consumed half.'* Many fine illuminated pages of parchment were just used as covers for account books and similar items. A mid fourteenth century map of the world from Creake Abbey is at the British Library, having been used as a cover for a rental. It is a fanciful production, with imaginative descriptions of tribes such as *'the Agofagy, who eat only panthers and lions and have one eye in their foreheads and large feet and are of deadly aspect'*. This, however, is a pre-Dissolution loss. The rental is of 1483-4 so the map was probably taken from the abbey at the time of the devastating fire there already discussed - in fact the rental it protects is of the property of Walter Aslak, one of those who came to the abbey's aid after the fire.

As well as richly illuminated manuscripts, the monks would also be working on the more mundane documents relating to the running to the monastic house itself. The most important of these would be the *cartulary*, or register copy of the title deeds of the monastery and its estates. These now survive for only 19 Norfolk houses (although there are extracts for two others - Carrow and Mountjoy - taken from now-lost originals). The Norfolk Record Office has cartularies for Norwich Cathedral priory and for five other houses - Coxford, Marham, St Benet's, North Creake and Pentney. The British Library have cartularies for 10 Norfolk houses, the Bodleian Library, Oxford for four, Cambridge libraries for three, and there is one at the Public Record Office. (This adds up to more than 19 because cartularies for some houses are scattered among more than one repository).

The other major series of monastic records are the account rolls compiled each year by each official of his receipts and expenses for the year. Where these survive they give a full picture of the detailed life of the monastery. In addition, a monastery would maintain the same records as were made by any lay lord - manor court rolls, bailiffs' accounts, rentals, surveys and leases of its property. These cannot be discussed here but again the survival rate for

Norfolk monasteries is by far the greatest for the two which were not totally dissolved - Norwich Cathedral priory and St Benet's Abbey. The transcription by David Yaxley of the inventories of the manor houses of Norwich Cathedral priory gives an excellent impression of what life was like in a medieval manor house, whether monastic or secular.

Although the monks must have thought about their faith and discussed it among themselves, evidence of what they thought is very rare indeed. At a visitation in 1514 the prior of Wymondham complained that his sacrist Richard Cambridge did not believe in the resurrection at the last day - was this a technical disagreement about theology or a case of a monk who had lost his faith?

ART

Apart from books, very few works of art survive from Norfolk monasteries. The best examples, naturally, are in the Cathedral priory. They include the stories from the Bible carved in the bosses of the roof of the Cathedral and the cloister. The details are derived from contemporary Norwich - in the Red Sea scene, Pharaoh rides a chariot very like a Norfolk cart and, in another scene, Joseph and Rebecca stand outside what looks like a typical fifteenth century Norwich house. The carving over the east door from the cloister to the Cathedral is a masterpiece of sculpture. The figures include a carving of Moses, portrayed with horns. This derives from a misunderstanding of a word in the Latin translation of the Bible. Moses is described as CORNATUM, which was meant to mean 'haloed' but was taken to mean 'horned'.

Another monastic treasure is the *retable*, or painted panel from behind an altar. Two beautiful retables from Norfolk monastic houses survive. That now in St Luke's chapel in Norwich Cathedral was perhaps made for the High Altar after damage to the previous one when the spire fell in 1362. After the Dissolution it was discarded: it has only survived because it was turned upside down and the back used as a table for over three hundred years. It was 'rediscovered' in 1847 and is one of the finest artistic works from medieval East Anglia.

The other retable is at Thornham Parva church, just over the Suffolk border. This was discovered in 1927 in a loft over a stable at Thornham Hall. The painting includes an image of St Dominic himself, and also of another Dominican saint, St Peter Martyr, so it seems clear that it originally came from a Dominican friary. Research into the painting during its restoration at

How they lived - daily life 85

the end of the twentieth century has established that it was almost certainly painted at Thetford Dominican friary. The basis for this identification lies in a combination of art history, archival and archaeological evidence. The style of the painting is that of East Anglian art in the 1330s. We know from archival evidence that Thetford Dominican priory was founded in 1335: the other Dominican friaries in the area are much earlier. The two people who gave the land for the Thetford house were John de Warenne and Edmund de Gonville: it is surely no coincidence that the saints on the painting include St John (the Baptist) and St Edmund. Finally, archaeological work at the Thetford site has uncovered over 300 fragments of stained glass from the friary windows, which are in the same style and with the same predominant colours as the retable. Therefore it deserves its place in this book as a Norfolk monastic treasure even though it is now in a Suffolk parish church.

A painter's palette has been found by archaeologists on the site of the Norwich Grey Friars. It was made from an oyster shell and contained several patches of paint - blue, red and brown. This large palette was probably used for the decoration of the church itself rather than manuscript work - however something very similar was no doubt used in creating the paintings that survive at Horsham St Faith priory and Yarmouth Franciscan friary which have already been mentioned.

44. The central portion of the Thornham Parva retable, originally painted for Thetford Dominican priory

DIET

There is no doubt that monks generally were well fed compared with many of their contemporaries. Dinner was of two courses and the food was intended to be so plentiful that the monks had no excuses for dining out at private houses or inns. Ale was the standard drink and a staple part of the monastic diet - a monk's diet might include eight pints a day: however the ale was very weak by modern standards. Stocktaking at the small Benedictine cell at Yarmouth in 1485 revealed 11 barrels of beer on the premises. Wine became more fashionable in later centuries and some monasteries even had their own vineyards: the monks of Norwich Cathedral priory were growing vines on their Sedgeford estate as early as the mid-thirteenth century: they brought the vine stock over from Ely. According to Walter Rye, St Benet's Abbey sold just under £6 worth of wine in one year. Cutlery was simple: spoons were provided, each monk using their own knife (forks were not used until the fifteenth century). At the cathedral priory each novice would purchase a drinking cup from the refectorer which he would use until he died: it would then be returned to the refectorer to be purchased by a new novice.

The Benedictine rule clearly prohibited the eating of meat from four-legged animals, except for the sick. However the abbot's table always provided meat for the lay guests, and monks might sometimes be invited to join them. By the early thirteenth century many monasteries had a second dining hall in which meat could be eaten. This was prohibited at several chapters from 1237 onwards but the practice continued at Norwich and elsewhere. In 1316 healthy monks were allowed to eat flesh-meat in the infirmary. By the fifteenth century it had become a custom to serve meat on at least three days a week except during Lent and Advent.

There would be special feasts on important days in the religious calendar. One sub-cellarer's account survives for St Winwaloy's priory in Wereham, covering the year 1351-2. It includes a list of saints' days and the hens or pullets purchased for them. On two occasions, including Christmas Eve, they bought 'wyldfowl' (their Latin appears to have failed them at this point as this is the only word in the account roll in English): it must have meant a pleasant Christmas feast for the monks in this small, isolated house. A single account roll also survives for Hempton priory. This dates from 1500-1 and the food being purchased by the priory includes beef, mutton, pork, eggs, chickens, mackerel, herrings and oysters.

Fish was always an important part of the monastic diet. Extra items of sea-food eaten during Lent at Hempton included salmon, turbot and mussels.

As we have seen, most monasteries had their own fish-ponds. The endowment at Mountjoy by its founder included 1,000 red herrings each Michaelmas. A recently discovered account roll from St Benet's records expenses on making nets, repairing a boat and cleaning out fishponds. According to Blomefield, the mason Ulmar gave Castle Acre 2,000 eels in Methwold 'for ever' In the early thirteenth century Ralph de Warren gave the same house two fishing boats on the mere at Saham. In 1306 there was a dispute between St Benet's and Lord Hugh de Veer about fishing rights in a stream called the Rendles in Potter Heigham: the abbey agreed to pay de Veer 12 shillings a year for the rights to the fish in the stream. When the priory at Hempton sold part of their fishery there to the local townsmen in 1436, they were clearly concerned with preservation of the stock: the townsmen were forbidden to fish with dragnets!

Originally the monastic estate provided the basic needs of the house - grain for flour and ale, peas and beans, fish, eggs, poultry, vegetables, herbs, wood and timber. In later centuries the estates were often simply rented out and the rental income used to purchase food from local shops and markets. David Dymond comments on the lack of fruit and vegetables (apart from onions) in the diet of Thetford Cluniac priory: perhaps they were not recorded because they were 'home-grown'?

Heads of houses ate separately from the monks and had a more generous diet: they were often entertaining important guests who would expect a good meal. This can be illustrated from the fate of the abbot of Wymondham after he was forced to resign in 1492. It was hardly one of privation. He was ordered to live at Downham Hall and three servants were provided for him. Every week the abbey had to supply them 18 loaves of best bread and 18 loaves of 'trencherd bread' (bread would be made of various qualities: the cheapest was black rye bread, which was fed to the poor). He was to have 18 flagons of customary ale every week. Each day he was to be given a dish of dinner and of supper of the best kind, as would serve for four monks. Another dish was to be provided for his servants. The abbey even had to pay for the maintenance of four horses for the former abbot and his men.

Of course it was not just the monks who had to be fed but all the servants and all the guests too. The number of servants would far outnumber the monks themselves. At Pentney in 1536 there were nine canons but also 83 other people - 23 hinds (estate labourers), 30 household servants and 30 children and other poor servants. In 1292 there were 44 servants at Blackborough.

R. H. Snape *(English Monastic Finance)* divides these servants into five groups:

1   artisans, smiths, carpenters, tilers, tailors and shoemakers
2   those engaged in the mill, bake-house and brewery
3   workers within the grounds - gardeners, pig-keepers, poultry-keepers
4   those at work in the stables and the messengers
5   servants within the house, the gate, the dining-room, kitchen, laundry, infirmary and church

The distinction between the servants and their holy masters was not always as absolute as might be supposed. At Walsingham in the early fifteenth century, a Mr Smith acted as caterer to the monastery while his wife bought fish for it in the local markets: she had the keys to most of the storerooms in the priory. Some of the canons allegedly used to eat and drink in the Smiths' house until eleven at night!

HEALTH

All monks would pass through the infirmary four times a year for blood-letting. This was believed to be necessary for good health and was also a relatively relaxed time for the monk. Jocelin of Brakelond says that at blood-letting time *'monks are wont to reveal to each other the secrets of the heart,*

45. Walsingham Austin priory: the dining room

How they lived - daily life 89

and to talk over matters with each other'. St Benedict himself allowed that sick monks might have flesh-meat so this was available in the infirmary even in the early days when it was not allowed in the main dining-room. The monastic houses, like the rest of Norfolk, must have suffered severely during the Black Death of 1349 but figures are impossible to come by. The number of monks at Norwich Cathedral priory may have been halved (the evidence for this is from the St Leonard's account roll: St Leonard's was accustomed to give each monk in the Cathedral priory a sum of money and the amount given suddenly drops by half). Hutton's book *The Franciscans in England* (1926) says that the entire community of Franciscan friars in Norwich was wiped out by the Black Death but there does not seem to be any documentary evidence for this. At Hickling (according to the Victoria County History) the prior died of plague and his successor very soon followed: only two canons survived the Black Death here, one of whom was appointed prior although he was technically still a novice.

Bishop Bateman's Register, which covers the period of the Black Death, suggests how badly many of the monastic houses were hit. The Bishop had to approve the appointment of new heads of religious houses in his diocese (which covered Suffolk as well as Norfolk). On average there were two such appointments a year through natural wastage. However in the single month of July 1349 no less than 11 new heads were appointed: presumably most, if not all, of the former heads had died of plague. Eight of the 11 houses were in Norfolk - Carrow, Crabhouse, Thetford St Sepulchre, Mountjoy, Wormegay, Hickling, Westacre and Walsingham. The register specifically says that at Mountjoy the prior and all the canons were dead - a canon from Wormegay was appointed prior instead. In the following month a new prior was appointed at Pentney. He also had to be brought in from outside (in this case from Letheringham in Suffolk) because there were no canons left suitable to be appointed prior - so presumably all the senior monks, at least, had died of plague.

The way in which the Black Death caused chaos is also suggested the records of the Cathedral infirmarer for 1349. An account roll was begun as usual at Michaelmas (1348). The official was Ralph de Swanton. However on 10 July 1349 John de Heders took over the account and his own last entry is at Christmas 1349: both officials had probably died of the plague. The roll ends with a note that 52s.1d. had been stolen from the infirmarer's office: clearly the organisation here had broken down completely. Work on the Cathedral cloisters came to a sudden stop on 25 June 1349: again this was probably because of the Black Death although this is never explicitly stated.

Henry Swinden, when working on the Great Yarmouth borough archives, noted that more wills occur among these records for 1349 than in any other year, again suggesting an unusually high mortality rate. He transcribed 23 of these wills. All but one left money to St Nicholas church and 18 asked to be buried there. The church was of course administered by the Benedictine monks, but these testators seem more interested in the parish church rather than the monastic institution: almost all the money bequeathed was for the fabric of the church and only one man left money for the monks themselves. The money was often specifically for the 'new work' extending the church to the west: this would have made the building by far the largest parish church in England, but it was abandoned soon after 1349, probably yet another consequence of the Black Death.

SANCTUARY

Monasteries would occasionally act as sanctuaries for criminals, as occurs in the Cadfael novels of Ellis Peters. When the citizens of Norwich hanged a petty thief called Walter Eghe in the Market Place in 1286 they bungled the job. His body was cut down and taken to the parish church of St George Tombland for burial. Here he revived: he could hardly be dragged out of the church so it was guarded by the local watch. After 15 days Eghe managed to evade them and escape across Tombland into the Cathedral priory. Here he could not be taken: the case went to the king and Eghe was eventually pardoned. The Dominican friary in the city was also a place of sanctuary. In 1365 three prisoners who broke out of Norwich Castle gaol fled there. Again they could not be forced out: the king fined the sheriff £15 for allowing the escape. The case in which the prioress of Carrow was imprisoned (described earlier) was also presumably partly a dispute about whether the priory was a place of sanctuary.

Two sanctuary cases at Yarmouth Black Friars indicate the cosmopolitan flavour of that town in the Middle Ages. John Scot hid there after breaking out of gaol, having stolen £30 worth of goods from merchants from Winchelsea and Flanders. Godfrey Gom also escaped from Yarmouth gaol to the Black Friars: he had murdered a man from Gascony. As was customary, both men were given fifteen days to leave the country. Medieval mercy was strictly limited however: if they did not leave, or if they returned to England, they would be summarily hanged

All was not always peaceful within the cloister itself. The Middle Ages appear to have been a time of hot-headedness and violent temper in general, both outside the cloister and within it. All monks carried knives as a matter of course. Even St Benedict accepted this, ordering that monks were to sleep in their habits 'but not with their knives at their sides as they sleep for the fear that a brother should be wounded while asleep'. There are many cases of monastic arguments leading to violence. In 1248, prior Stephen of Thetford had a disagreement with a Welsh monk who had just arrived there from Cluny: the monk drew his knife and killed the prior outside the church door. Another prior to be murdered by one of his brethren was Humphrey of Weybridge priory who, according to the gaol delivery rolls, was killed by a canon called Robert in 1308: nothing is known of the background to the case. In 1317 one of the canons at Beeston attacked and wounded the Bishop of Norwich himself: the canon was sent to Rome for punishment but eventually absolved. In 1491 a canon of Langley cut off the hand of a friar during an argument.

LEISURE

As the inhabitants of monastic houses became more sophisticated, they found more time for pleasurable pursuits. Our evidence for these mainly occurs in complaints made at visitations by bishops of the monastic houses in their dioceses. These were never complete: friars lay outside the visitation of the Bishop, as did the larger exempt abbeys and the houses of the Cistercians, Carthusians and white canons. The latter, however, were inspected throughout England by Bishop Redman in the last quarter of the fifteenth century.

Archbishop Peckham, himself a Franciscan friar, visited many monastic houses in Norwich diocese in 1280-1. He was at Coxford in 1281 and subsequently wrote a letter to the prior giving him a severe dressing-down. Thanks to the prior's laxity, the canons went coursing with hounds, played chess and other games, chatted with girls and made the house a laughing-stock in the neighbourhood. However 200 years later the canons were complaining to Bishop Goldwell that no honest recreation was provided. In the cloister at Norwich Cathedral priory, holes for games like Nine Men's Morris can still be seen on the stone benches, reflecting the increase in leisure pursuits as centuries passed. They also remind us of a complaint by one of the senior Norwich Cathedral priory monks at a visitation enquiry that the younger brothers 'do nothing but play cards and dice here'. Entertainment at Thetford Cluniac priory included visits by musicians, minstrels, jugglers and actors. The monks hunted foxes and watched exotic animals: they saw men with bears and twice a man with a camel. Interestingly, the priory also contributed to plays and games held in the town and in neighbouring villages.

Some of the complaints in the fifteenth and sixteenth centuries suggest pretty lax behaviour in several monastic houses. After a visitation in 1486 the canons of Langley were given orders forbidding them to hunt and fish at night! In 1520 the Bromehill canons were told not to frequent taverns and not to leave the monastery without the permission of their superior. The prior of St Benet's was accused of rushing away after matins to go hunting!

As we have seen, the male and female inhabitants of Shouldham each in effect had their own monasteries built around their own cloister greens. Life seems to have been relatively relaxed and to have included informal games of football! We know this because in 1321 a man died during such a game: he ran up against one of the canons, William de Spalding, and was stabbed by a knife that William was wearing under his monastic robe. William was stricken with guilt and remorse and the case was considered by the Pope himself: in the end his Holiness decided it was a pure accident and no one was to blame.

The occasional bit of poaching no doubt provided both fun and food. Walter Rye quotes two examples, both revealing monastic inventiveness. The canons of North Creake were once fined £10 for poaching rabbits on Burnham Common: they were using 'furrets, hooks, nets and engines'. In 1446 a servant from Walsingham priory was caught using 'harepypes' to take rabbits from the same warren.

HOW THEY LIVED - INCOME AND EXPENDITURE

INCOME - SPIRITUALITIES

Apart from gifts and bequests, the income of a religious house derived from three or four sources. The two main ones were the *spiritualities* - money from churches - and the *temporalities* - money from land. The other two possible sources were donations from pilgrims (in those houses lucky enough to have relics worth coming to look at) and from those people wishing to be buried in the church or cemetery of the monastery.

The idea of making a profit out of a church is not easy for the modern mind to grasp but it was a familiar one in the Middle Ages. It goes back to the beginnings of the parish system. In England most parish churches were 'proprietary' churches, that is they were in effect owned by the person who founded them, who might be a clergyman or a layman. He would receive the profit from the church in the form of the income deriving from it. He could sell his rights in the church just like any other property.

In very early days it was simply left to individuals to decide what they wanted to give to their local church. By the eleventh century, however, this had become systemised. They were to give a *tithe*, that is a tenth of the crops they grew and the stock they raised. This included the fishing harvest: the Cathedral priory, as patrons of St Nicholas Yarmouth, claimed the tithe of all fish brought into the harbour. One tenth of everybody's produce could well be a large amount in total, much larger that one person could use - hence the huge tithe barns to store it in, like the ones that still can be seen at Wacton and Paston. This meant that the average parish church was a profit-making institution. What the rector could do was to take the profits himself and put in a *vicar* or substitute. The vicar would receive a fixed stipend and be responsible for the day to day religious life of the people. It was the vicar who performed the religious services, baptised, married and buried the parishioners, who gave blessings as asked and who administered the Holy Sacrament. The rector would take the bulk of the profits and do almost nothing. He did have a few responsibilities of course, such as keeping the chancel in good repair. (The parishioners were responsible for the nave. As they usually took more pride in their local church than did the rector, it is common to find a grand and lavishly decorated nave with an older and plainer chancel tacked on to it.) The rector was also responsible for the upkeep of the cemetery and had some duties towards the poor of the parish.

46. Thetford St Mary: infirmary cloister

We have called the rector 'he' but for many churches the rector was an 'it' - a religious house. From Saxon times onwards many churches were *appropriated*, that is given, to monasteries. It might be thought that the monks or canons would act as the local parish priest in these churches. This happened fairly often with white canons and sometimes with the black canons - the churches of Buckenham All Saints (now the parish church) and St Andrew (now gone) for example had canons from the local priory acting as their parish priests. Canons at Westacre served the parish church which lies beside the gatehouse of their precinct. This happened very rarely with the monks however (and of course could not happen with the nuns) - to them, and to most of the canons too, the churches that were appropriated by them were simply sources of income. Bromholme, for example, owned churches in Burgh Castle and Warham and Castle Acre owned churches as far away as Essex and Yorkshire. Monks would not be travelling to give services in these district parishes: a vicar would be paid to do this and the monastery would simply take the profits. Another example is that of Creake abbey. The abbey owned churches at Hapton, Gateley, Quarles, and Great Ringstead and had a half-share in the church at Wreningham. The latter was sold by them in 1414, illustrating clearly that churches were treated like any other property, to be bought and sold at will. A group of Norfolk churches including Costessey were actually owned by the monastery of Bon Repos in France: the French house leased the churches not to a Norfolk monastery but to the Cistercian house of Sawtry in Huntingdonshire. (Sawtry did have a Norfolk presence, with a cell at Prior's Thorns in Swaffham, so the situation was not quite as bizarre as it might appear.)

Twenty five percent of all parish churches in England had passed from lay hands to religious hands by 1200 and the figure had risen to one third by 1300. By the fifteenth century almost all of Norwich's 60 or so parish churches were owned by religious bodies of various kinds, half of them by the Cathedral priory. To give a church to a monastery was a relatively easy way of ensuring one's passage to heaven, being less painful to the family status than giving away landed estates. Even so there were cases of heirs trying to claim back from religious houses churches that their ancestors had given away. A Binham charter of about 1140 said that if an heir withdrew his father's gift he was failing his father by destroying the bridge that he had built to paradise. Many gifts, of course, were made out of devotion rather than out of fear. Gunnora, the wife of Robert de Essex, gave three churches to Thetford Cluniac priory in gratitude for the safe delivery of her son, Henry. Gunnora was the daughter of Roger Bigot, so this is another example of different generations of a family favouring a monastery they no doubt saw as in some sense their own.

Although appropriation could undoubtedly be seen as an abuse, and was seen in this way by many contemporaries, it was not always a bad thing. Many other parishes had rectors who were *pluralist* (held several parishes) or *non-resident* (did not live in the parish): these could suffer from a lack of personal pastoral care as much as the parish churches appropriated to monasteries. A religious house might be expected to have at least some concern for the spiritual lives of the parishioners who attended their churches, and to make an effort to ensure a steady flow of decent vicars. No doubt this did often happen but the unfortunate fact is that the stipend that a vicar received was so low that there were many better-paid jobs in the clerical world for able priests. This made it unlikely that the best - or at least the best educated - men would serve as a vicar if other employment was available for him. However some churches did gain directly from monastic ownership. Trowse church has a fine east window of the 1270s, designed by no less an artist than the mason of Norwich Cathedral himself. This is because the church was owned by the Cathedral priory who were therefore responsible for the maintenance of the chancel.

Nuns owned churches too. Carrow was given four churches in Norwich by its founder King Stephen - All Saints, St Julian, St Edward and St Catherine (also known as St Winwaloy). In 1249 they were given the advowson of Earlham together with 26 acres of land there. They later acquired the advowson of Wroxham along with the manor. The parochial church of St James at Carrow itself was also theirs - this building was demolished in the sixteenth century. When the advowson of Surlingham was acquired by Carrow priory, the vicar's portion of tithes was described in terms typical of those given in cases of appropriation. The vicar was to have tithes of hay, wool, milk, flax and hemp, foals, calves, lambs, pigs, eggs, chickens, hens and doves, geese, swans, ducks, honey and wax, apples, peas and any fruit of the trees of gardens, offerings from mills, fish ponds, wood and turf stacks. These tithes were known as the lesser tithes in contrast to the greater tithes (usually corn, hay and wood) which almost invariably went to the monastic house. The minor tithes would have been more time-consuming to collect, of course, and only someone living on the spot could expect to be able to enforce the collection of them.

47. Westacre: All Saints parish church and the monastary gatehouse

INCOME - TEMPORALITIES

For some religious houses the spiritualities were the main source of income, for others the temporalities were more profitable. In 1292 Blackborough was getting half of its income from its estates and half from its churches - £10 from St Martin Raynham, £5.6s.8d. from Middleton and £5 from their half-share in the church at Wetherden (Suffolk). Whenever a religious house was founded, the founder would give it land enough for it to be self-sufficient in food and other produce. (The friaries were a exception to this, at first, as they were not intended to own any land at all: their food and other needs were to be met by begging.) Other people might give further land to the monastery, or leave it land in their wills. Once the monastery had capital of its own, it might well choose to invest it in land. This pattern can be seen at Bromehill, a relatively late foundation. It was founded in the early thirteenth century and surviving charters from that date record gifts to it of small pieces of nearby land for the saving of the souls of the donors and their relatives. However by the end of the century it was buying land: it was granted six acres in Ickworth not only for the soul of the donor but also for giving him nine marks of silver.

The immense importance of the monasteries as landowners can be seen in the fact that at the Dissolution it was generally supposed that one third of all land in England was owned by them. This may have been a slight exaggeration but a quarter seems a reasonable estimate. T. H. Swales estimates that 219 manors and 171 churches in Norfolk were owned by religious houses at the Dissolution (and this presumably excludes the 35 manors and 16 churches formerly owned by St Benet's which had already passed to the Bishop of Norwich). Some small houses, especially the nunneries, might just own land within the village in which they were situated, and perhaps one or two neighbouring parishes. Medium sized monasteries might have land scattered through one or two dozen parishes. Flitcham had land in eight Norfolk parishes in 1291, Blackborough in 25, Wendling in 29 and Hempton in about 40. The largest houses owned much more: Westacre had property in 74 Norfolk parishes, St Benet's in over 70 and the Cathedral priory in over 100. Many Norfolk monastic houses also had lands in other counties too: West Dereham, for example, had property in Yorkshire and the Cathedral priory had land in Kent as well as extensive estates in Suffolk. In the same way, several monasteries from outside Norfolk had estates within the county - Bury St Edmunds had land in 50 Norfolk parishes and Ramsey Abbey in over 30. As might be expected, most of these monasteries were in the nearby counties of Suffolk, Cambridgeshire and Lincolnshire. However a few were much further away - Tintern Abbey in Monmouthshire owned the right to present to Halvergate church.

So much land was passing into the ownership of monasteries and other institutions that from Magna Carta onwards laws were passed to prevent land going to the 'dead hand' of the church, culminating in the Statute of Mortmain of 1279. From this date, a licence was needed from the king before a monastery or any other corporation could acquire a new piece of land - and of course a fee had to be paid. These licences were recorded on the patent rolls so that our knowledge of monastic acquisitions is much greater after this date: unfortunately the great days of giving to monastic houses had long passed. Sometimes the licences themselves survive too - the Norfolk Record Office has a group of four licences relating to Mountjoy in Haveringland for example. In this case the estates being acquired by this small house was acquiring were very local - in Haveringland itself and in the nearby villages of Cawston, Swannington, Felthorpe and Irmingland. The acquisitions included the advowson of Irmingland church.

Monasteries might sell land, of course, or exchange pieces of land with other landowners, whether laymen or other religious institutions. This would normally be done to rationalise their holdings and make them more economically viable. In 1380, Norwich cathedral priory gave its church at Chalk in Kent to Cobham College, receiving in return the College's manor in Martham. This must have made economic sense to both parties, especially as the cathedral priory already owned a large amount of land in Martham. Monasteries might also rent land on occasion: in 1306 Molycourt rented three acres of land in Outwell from John, son of Gilbert. The rent was twelve pence a year and the lease was for the extraordinarily long term of 2,000 years: probably this little house did not have the cash simply to buy the land outright.

Monastic houses were the lords of many Norfolk manors. They held manorial courts and received fines and fees from their tenants. In the early Middle Ages, they also had

48. Trowse parish church: the east window designed by the Norwich Cathedral priory mason

the right of direct labour from their tenants for certain times, as described in the custumal of the manor. These customs would vary enormously from manor to manor but would usually include the duties of harvesting the lord's corn and hay and carting it to his barns. They might also have to give him a fixed amount of their produce such as chickens and eggs. The lord would often provide meals during these periods - the evidence seems to be that monastic lords tended to be slightly more generous than lay lords, in this respect at least. Some villages might have several monastic landlords - of the 18 manors in Worstead, six were owned by religious houses. All three manors in East Rudham were owned by monasteries - Coxford, Castle Acre and Horsham St Faith.

Monastic houses used their estates in exactly the same way as any other landowner of the time. At first they grew produce for themselves and brought it to their house for their consumption. However, increasingly through the Middle Ages, they would rent out part or all of their estates and live off the rental income. The small alien priory of Toft Monks, for example, had estates in Warwickshire, Berkshire and Dorset. An inventory of the effects on these estates made in 1374 shows that they were farmed out to a George Felbrigg: he would have paid the monastery a set amount each year and hope to make a profit for himself. The inventory gives a good idea of what a small monastic grange would be like. In the hall or main room there was an attempt at comfort with a tapestry and six cushions. A cup made partly of silver and six silver spoons were kept in the cellar and no doubt produced for important guests. More basic equipment was kept in the kitchen including six 'worn and broken' brass pans and 12 pewter dishes. This small farm was a mixed one - at the time of the inventory the stock included one bull, three cows and three sucking calves. There were also six oxen for ploughing.

Sheep farming was a form of agriculture especially associated with the Cistercians and white canons but very common with other orders too. In 1514 Bromehill had more than 2,000 sheep. Thetford St Mary had grazing for at least 7,000 sheep and Horsham St Faith grazing for 3,000 sheep just on its land in Hellesdon. The Cathedral priory also had enormous flocks of sheep on its estate in north west Norfolk. Too much dependence on sheep could lead to problems: many monasteries suffered financial problems in the 1290s as a result of an outbreak of sheep scab.

Some of the monastic estates may have seemed easy targets for thieves - and jurors may have looked sympathetically at such thefts. The gaol delivery rolls for Norfolk for the ten-year period 1307 and 1316 have been printed by Barbara Hanawalt. They make interesting reading. Eight men were accused over this period of stealing sheep from monastic flocks. Three were found guilty and hanged. (In the Middle Ages there were no custodial sentences: if you were convicted you were executed.) Four others were acquitted and one man refused to plead. However all the men found guilty had stolen from laymen as well as from monasteries whereas the three acquitted had only stolen from religious houses, suggesting a possible feeling that stealing sheep just from monasteries was not considered a very serious act. There were other kinds of theft too - two men broke into houses owned by monasteries to steal clothing while four men broke into monastic barns to steal barley or oats. These people were probably starving: all six cases occurred in 1315 and 1316, which were years of desperate famine in England. In the case of one man, Thomas Swan, who stole a tunic from the house of the abbot of St Benet's at Shotesham, it is explicitly recorded that he *'did it because he was hungry and destitute'*. The jurors may have felt the same way about the other accused: five of the six men were acquitted and the sixth was only returned to prison because the jury in his case had failed to appear.

The monasteries had many sources of income other than land. Many of them owned watermills or windmills: people brought their corn to be ground to flour, on payment of a fee of course. Norwich Cathedral priory had no less than three mills in the village of Hindolveston for example. Mills were very desirable sources of income: in the thirteenth century the Cathedral priory purchased one at Southwood for 100 shillings. In the middle of that century the same priory paid £10 for a watermill and windmill at Thornham (and agreed to pay the former owner, the Bishop of Norwich, 40 shillings a year). Castle Acre owned Bridge Mill, just to the west of Fakenham Mill: it leased it to the nearby priory at Hempton. There were continual disputes between the monastic houses and Fakenham manor, because the mills were so close together: the monastic mill had the great advantage of being upstream. The arguments were not only about the flow of water but also about public access over the Wensum: as this was the main route for pilgrims approaching Walsingham from the south, both parties in the dispute were probably hoping to attract trade from passing pilgrims.

Not all mills were for grinding corn: others might be used for *fulling*. This was the process of cleaning and thickening cloth by beating it while it was in water. Fulling involved hard manual labour and this effort might be saved by harnessing the energy of a mill to do the work. Norwich Cathedral priory had a fulling mill at Eaton, just outside Norwich: in 1473 it leased it to John Boydon who was to keep it in repair with timber from the priory wood there. Thetford Cluniac priory also had a fulling mill: this was at Syleham in Suffolk.

How they lived - income and expenditure 101

Another form of income was that from woodland. Woods brought in income from timber (for building), from underwood (for fuel) and also from the mast (beech-nuts) and acorns: villagers would pay to be allowed to feed their pigs on these in the winter. The Cathedral's wood at Hindolveston is a well-recorded one. In 1335 it is called Hilderston Wode, presumably reflecting the local pronunciation of the name. In the late twelfth century a bank and fence three miles long was erected around the wood and a woodward employed to protect it: the produce was mainly underwood rather than timber. In the fourteenth century the wood was leased to a man who made hurdles. His name was John Robynes and it somehow became attached to the wood, which was known as Robins Wood for at least 400 years.

A major source of income for a monastic or lay lord was to be allowed to run a market or fair. Many monasteries were granted these rights - the monks of Norwich for example ran the fair in Tombland just outside their gates. A dispute at this fair in 1272 blew up into a full-scale riot: the angry citizens of Norwich attacked the priory, setting fire to its roof and destroying many of its documents. Another disputed fair was Bromehill where local priory and the borough of Thetford both claimed the rights: however, as the priory resigned their claim in return for an annual payment of eighteen pence, this fair cannot have produced much profit. Wymondham priory ran the weekly market in the town and also a three-day fair each year. In 1199 King John granted West Dereham a weekly market at Dereham and also a four-day yearly fair, 'with toll, tallage and liberties belonging'. Even a small priory like Hempton had two fairs and a market: the cattle fairs at Hempton survived well into the nineteenth century. Bromholme had a weekly market and also an annual fair, which naturally enough was held upon the day of the Exaltation of the Holy Cross when there would be very many pilgrims around. One of the few known facts about the nuns at Lyng is that they held a yearly fair in the village: they continued to own this fair even after their move to Thetford.

There was a wide range of other economic activities too. Carbrooke owned a dovecote which raised 6s.8d. a year. The sub-prior of Westacre was said in 1494 to be more interested in rabbit farming and swan rearing than he was in his devotions. Thetford Cluniac priory had warren lodges for rabbits: one of these, now known as Thetford Warren Lodge, still survives (although damaged by fire in 1935). Both Beeston and Bromholme priories had right of wreck along the nearby coast - in 1415 Bromholme received 3s.8d. as a fine from a man who had taken a barrel of butter he found on the beach. The Cathedral priory and St Benet's both had swan pits: that at the latter can still be seen. They reared swans and their beaks were marked with symbols to show which swans were theirs. Other priories such as Ingham and Carrow had swan marks too: the Norfolk Record Office has a recently discovered Swan Roll from the late fifteenth century which shows just how many religious institutions of all kinds owned swans in the Broadland area of the county alone. This area boasted other forms of produce: the Cathedral priory, for example, owned a good deal of marshland in Raveningham, Rockland, Surlingham and elsewhere. The reeds would be used for thatching and also for strewing over the floor of the church. Salt was an important product from salt marshes - Horsham St Faith obtained salt from its marshes at Mautby, near Caister on Sea.

Monastic lords also led the way in draining marshes in the Fens and the in area west of Yarmouth. This created rich - and profitable - arable and pasture land. Originally many monastic houses had been deliberately founded in

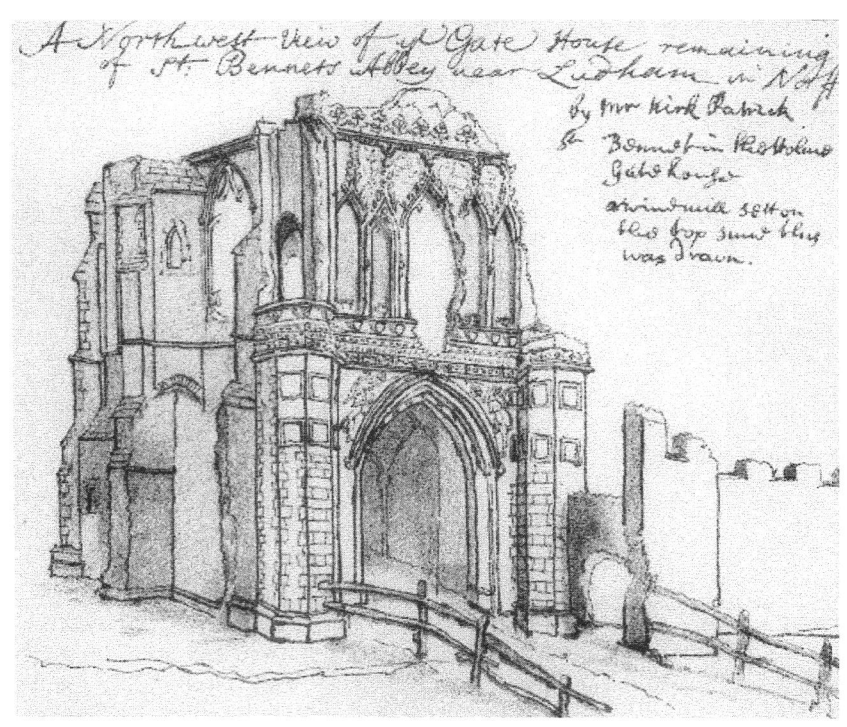

49. St Benet's abbey: the gatehouse drawn by John Kirkpatrick in the early 18th century, shortly before it was made into a windmill (NRO, RYE 17 vol. 6)

inhospitable places. Slevesholm was on an island in the fens. Blomefield says that it was also known as 'Slush-holm', a name that may suggest the marshy nature of the ground. Crabhouse was founded on the bank of the Ouse at a place called Bustard's Dole which (according to the cartulary) was 'all wild and far around on every side was no human habitation'. The site was subject to flooding. The cartulary also describes some land here as newly recovered from water. It was the dedication and hard work of the monastic house that turned these unpromising sites into profitable farming estates. Traces of these improvements show up among the title deeds recorded in the Blackborough cartulary. A clergyman called Samson gave the convent 'our part in the marsh of Tilney which William Bek surrounded with a ditch'. Deeds relating to land owned by Lewes priory in Walpole and other marshland parishes include references to maintaining and repairing drains and sewers.

However, if the monastic house was too poor to invest in its estates, then the land would decrease in value rather than increase. By the mid fifteenth century Molycourt's lands had been so ruined by continual flooding that there was barely enough produce to sustain a single monk! The isolation of many religious houses can still be visualised at sites like Wormegay or Langley: all the fields between the house and the river at the latter site would have been marsh before they were drained to make highly fertile farmland. St Benet's is another isolated site: it was originally on an island and even now the easiest approach is by water. This is how the Bishop of Norwich arrives, when holding his annual service here on the first Sunday in August. The last Saxon abbot was actually entrusted with the defence of the coast by King Harold in 1066. There were many cases of flooding here: in the winter of 1287-8 all the outbuildings were under water and the abbey's horses had to be housed in the nave of the church!

Not all monastic land was in the countryside. Many houses had property in towns or cities, which they would rent out. Norwich Cathedral priory had many plots of land in the city including several market stalls. Monastic establishments might also need a house in Norwich on the occasions when the abbot or prior had to visit the city on his monastery's business. The abbots of Wendling and both had houses on King Street, the prior of Bromholme on Fishergate and the prior of Walsingham on Colegate (where the Woolpack inn now stands). In 1286 nine 'distant' monastic houses owning tenements in Norwich were reported not to have appeared before the Justices in Eyre as they should have done. Eight were Cistercian houses in the Midlands and Southern England, the ninth was the Gilbertine house at Chicksands in Bedfordshire. Their Norwich properties were presumably

50. Thetford Warren Lodge photographed during the fire of 1 August 1935 (NRO, MC 365/150)

bases for their extensive wool trading businesses. In the same way, Norfolk religious houses might have property in other cities: when Geoffrey Fitzpiers founded Shouldham he gave it a block of houses in London.

Another source of income in an economy largely based on water-transport was ownership of a quay (very often known as a staithe in Norfolk): fees would be charged for loading and unloading goods. The Abbot of Wendling owned the Quay called the Common Staithe in Norwich: in 1379 he leased it to the city for 600 years. Great Yarmouth Franciscan friary owned the stretch of quay in Yarmouth in front of the friary. The stone footings of the staithe at St Benet's can still be seen alongside the river and the marshy area just outside the monastery gate was originally a small dock. No doubt these facilities were primarily for the monastery's own use but goods sold at the two annual fairs held here would probably also have been loaded and unloaded.

INCOME - RELICS AND PILGRIMS

Many monastic houses held relics which pilgrims would travel to see, hoping that contact with a precious and holy object would bring them blessings. Physically and mentally handicapped people would be brought by their relatives in the hope of a cure.

The most visited house in Norfolk by far was Walsingham. This was one of the great pilgrimage places of Europe. We have already mentioned the Holy

How they lived - income and expenditure 105

House, the chief object of veneration to pilgrims. This was in a chapel on the north side of the priory church. The chapel had been built around the holy house and must have been awe-inspiring, with gold and jewels glittering in the candlelight. The other internationally famous object in the priory was the statue of Our Lady of Walsingham: this presumably resembled the image of it on the surviving priory seal.

Walsingham had two more treasures to tempt pilgrims. It had a reliquary containing milk from the breasts of the Blessed Virgin Mary. This lived on the High Altar. Erasmus saw it when he visited Walsingham in the early sixteenth century. He later wrote of it *'you would take it for beaten chalk tempera with the white of an egg'*. As if all this was not enough, the priory also had a finger of St Peter: this was kept in a chapel built between the two holy wells in the priory grounds already mentioned.

51. Walsingham Austin priory seal
(from Victoria County History*)*

Our first known pilgrim to Walsingham was Henry II who was there in 1226: the shrine must already have been of national importance for him to pay a visit. Henry II then went on to Bromholme, a pattern of pilgrimage no doubt repeated thousands of times over the next three centuries by people of all classes.

The priory of Bromholme was not quite in the same league as Walsingham, but it was not far behind: it was one of the most visited shrines in England. The relic here was the Holy Cross of Bromholme. According to legend, it was made of wood from the cross on which Jesus was crucified. This was found by St Helen, mother of the Roman emperor Constantine, when she visited Jerusalem in the early fourth century. She gave part of it to her son and it passed down through successive generations of emperors in Constantinople for almost a thousand years. It was a very powerful relic and the emperors carried it with them into battle. In 1205 the Emperor Baldwin failed to do this - he was defeated, captured and killed. When not at war, the relic was kept in the Emperor's church in Constantinople. Matthew Paris tells the story of how it came to Bromholme. One of the priests in the Emperor's entourage was a Norfolk man named Hugh (an interesting example of the international nature of the medieval Christian church). When the Emperor died, Hugh seized his opportunity - he stole the Cross and brought it to England, arriving in 1223. He then offered it to any monastery that would accept his sons as monks. Some religious houses refused, but Bromholme agreed to his terms. The gamble paid off - thousands of pilgrims came to see this wonder over the next three centuries including Henry III and Edward II.

Many other churches had pieces of wood thought to be part of the True Cross - they included Norwich Cathedral priory and Wendling abbey among the monasteries discussed in this book. However that at Bromholme was exceptional - not only was it unusually large (about the length of a man's hand) but it actually had on it the blood of Our Lord. It had been that part of the Cross *'which was most besprinkled with His blood'*. The relic is mentioned in two of the greatest poems of Medieval England. In Chaucer's Canterbury Tales, the Reeve's Tale includes the line:

Help, Holy Cross of Bromholme

The Vision of Piers Plowman also refers to it:

And bid the Rood of Bromholme
Bring me out of debt.

According to John Capgrave, the relic restored the sight of 19 blind people and no less than 39 people were raised from the dead after their corpses were brought in to the priory church. At the Dissolution, the Cross passed to Robert Southwell who gave it to the former prior of Pentney. This was Robert Codde who later became warden of the Great Hospital in Norwich. Presumably he took it to London to be destroyed in the great bonfires of relics that took place in Smithfield after the Dissolution.

The shrine about which we know the most is that of St William of Norwich. This is because one of the monks at the Cathedral, Thomas of Monmouth, wrote down the details of all the supposed miracles that took place at his tomb. William was a twelve-year old boy found murdered on Mousehold Heath in 1144. Somehow the absurd story got around that he had been ritually killed by members of the Norwich Jewish community. William's body was at first buried in the monk's cemetery at the Cathedral priory. William of Monmouth, after a series of visions, persuaded the authorities to move the body into the Chapter House, then (in 1151) to a place before the

High Altar in the Cathedral and finally (in 1154) into the Jesus Chapel. The miracles recorded by William took place at St William's tomb between 1150 and 1170: there were over a hundred of them. Most of them involved local people (over half lived within 20 miles of Norwich) so it was never a shrine of national importance like Bromholme or Walsingham. It was also relatively short-lived as a major curative shrine. At first there was a miracle every 10 days or so but by the 1160s they had declined to one or two a year. The cult never completely died out however - small sums continued to be received at his shrine and there are paintings of St William on some fifteenth century church screens such as at Loddon.

The Cathedral priory had other treasures. It was dedicated to the Holy Trinity and had statues of them on its high altar. In 1404 the priory spent the large sum of £12 for a jewel to adorn the body of Christ. In 1505 they paid a goldsmith 22s.10d. for making the shoes of the Holy Trinity. Many other religious houses had relics. St Benet's had the bones of two saints - Wolfric, the first hermit of the site, and Margaret, a martyr killed in Hoveton St John in 1170. Margaret is a good example of a local saint who has almost, but not quite, disappeared from memory. Our only documentary source is William Worcester: he writes that:

St Margaret the Martyr was killed in Little Wood in the hamlet of Hoveton St John AD 1170 ... on 2 May and lies buried beneath the high altar among the relics of the sacred abbey church.

William does not say who killed her or why she was considered a saint. St Benet's had property in Hoveton, so Margaret may well have been a tenant of the abbey. Interestingly, the Little Wood survives as a place-name 650 years later, appearing on the tithe map as the name of a field: presumably the wood itself had long ago been converted to pasture-land. This field, at the crossing north of the farm now called Two Saints Farm, has hawthorn hedges: the oak trees contained within these hedges could be descendants of trees that witnessed Margaret's martyrdom here over 800 years ago.

When Conrad became abbot of St Benet's in 1126 he brought with him from Canterbury a chalice made by St Dunstan himself, together with other relics. The Cluniac priory at Thetford had a wide range of sacred objects, whose discovery was in itself miraculous. When a wooden image of the Virgin in the priory was about to be repainted it was found to be hollow and to contain many relics, all fortunately labelled. They included part of Jesus' robe, a piece of the manger where he was born, and part of the gravecloth that Lazarus was wearing when he was resurrected.

Other important relics in Norfolk monastic houses included a foot of St Lucy the Virgin at Wendling. Castle Acre had an arm of St Philip: when the house surrendered in November 1536 the monks of the Cluniac priory at Thetford rushed to Castle Acre to rescue it and add it to their own treasury. St Leonard's priory in Norwich attracted many pilgrims with its jewel-covered statue of St Leonard and an image of King Henry VI which was reputed to have powers of healing. Even a tiny house like Molycourt might have a precious relic: there was an image of John the Baptist here. We know of it because Margaret, the wife of Thomas de Beaupres asked to be buried in front of it in her will of 1439.

Sums obtained from offerings at relics could be enormous. We have figures from the valuation of 1535, by which time the fashion for relics had declined to some extent. Walsingham was in a league of its own, of course. The chapel of Our Lady (where the house and statue were) received £250.1s.; the sacred milk of Our Lady 42s.3d.; and the church of St Lawrence (where St Peter's finger was) £8.9s.1½d. - a grand total of £260 in one year. Offerings at the cross at Bromholme came to £5.12s.9d. However a surviving account roll for Bromholme dated 1415-6 shows that offerings then were much higher - £32.4s.5d. Less famous relics attracted smaller but substantial offerings: the arm of St Philip at Castle Acre was bringing in offerings of ten shillings a year in the 1530s.

It is, of course, easy to mock all this and to make sarcastic remarks about the number of pieces of the True Cross or feet of St Lucy that there were in churches throughout Europe. This is to miss the point. The fact that pilgrimages to relics were so popular shows that they fulfilled a need. In an age of unknown powers, uncertain and short lives, pilgrimages provided a purpose. As David Freedberg wrote 'fundamental to every pilgrimage is the element of hope. The focus of every pilgrimage journey is the shrine. The journeys are undertaken in the expectation, however weak of physical and spiritual benefits'. The journey to a shrine was like the journey through life to death and to the future life. The sight of a relic of a saint or biblical episode must also have brought the stories that were heard in church every Sunday vividly to life.

INCOME - BURIALS

The church expected people to die well, to be fit for their place in heaven. To many the medieval vision of heaven seems dull, with angels playing on harps, but once again we need to understand how people saw things at the time. They expected heaven to be a joy. Margery Kempe, the Lynn mystic,

How they lived - income and expenditure

had a vision of the music played there and cried out *'Alas that I ever did sin, it is full merry in heaven'*. A contrast was drawn in people's minds between the confusion of Hell (all too like the confusion in everyday medieval life) and the order of heaven - perhaps like the order in a monastic house. Julian of Norwich wrote about death: *'I saw a body lying on the earth which appeared heavy and horrible and without shape or form, as it were a swollen pit of stinking mud, and suddenly out of this body there sprung a most beautiful creature, a little child, fully shaped and formed, swift and lively and whiter than a lily, which quickly glided up to heaven'*. It was in this spirit that many people found an especial strength in being buried in a monastic house. This of course brought in money, including that of the mortuary.

We have already discussed burials in nunneries and friaries. Although the monasteries were not quite so popular, they had their devotees too, especially the founders or patrons and their families. Lady Margaret Foliot, as patroness of Wendling, was buried near to the high altar of the church. The Cluniac Priory of Thetford became in effect the family burial vault of the Duke of Norfolk in the early sixteenth century. In 1524 Thomas, the second Duke, died in his castle at Framlingham, Suffolk. His body was carried to Thetford followed by over 900 mourners. A knight on horseback was led down the nave of the priory church, his battleaxe held downwards. The body was laid in a vault in front of the high altar after which his officers broke their staves and threw them into the grave. The funeral was said to have cost £1,340.

When the Dissolution was imminent, the then Duke of Norfolk tried to turn Thetford priory into a collegiate chapel and family mausoleum. Henry VIII would not allow this, so the Duke had his ancestors' bones - taken from Thetford. They were put into the church at Framlingham which became the family mausoleum instead. Only the brick vault of the tomb now survives at Thetford as a reminder of this glorious funeral.

Other important people buried in Norfolk religious houses included Sir John Fastolf at St Benet's Abbey, and Richard, Earl of Gloucester (died 1261) and William de Ufford, Earl of Suffolk (died 1382), both buried at the Austin friary at Gorleston. When Sir John Paston died in London in 1466, his body was brought to Bromholme for burial. He left 40 shillings to the prior and 6s.8d. to each of the monks. This was another extravagant funeral: the funeral feast included the provision of 13 barrels of beer, 27 barrels of ale, 15 gallons of wine, 41 pigs and 49 calves.

Sir John's son (also Sir John) requested in his will of 1477 that he too be buried at Bromholme and also that a monument be erected over the tomb of this father there 'like no other in Norfolk'. In the event, however, Sir John junior died suddenly in London and was buried there. It is possible that the tomb-chest designed for his father survives: a tomb in Paston church, supposedly originally from Bromholme priory, could well be that of John Paston. Not all the Paston family favoured Bromholme, however: Clement Paston and Margery Paston (Sir John junior's wife, who died in 1495) both chose burial in the Norwich Carmelite friary.

Lesser men might also chose burial in a monastic house. William Martenet (died 1438), formerly vicar of Sporle, and John Spicer of Lynn (died 1440) both requested burial in Lynn Austin friary, for example. Martenet named the exact spot - he wanted burial in the chapel under the bell-tower. People like this no doubt had connections with the house in their lifetime: Spicer was actually living at the friary at the time of his death, even though he had a wife and a house elsewhere in Lynn.

Elizabeth Felmingham is another example of someone choosing to be buried in a friary. She had married twice, first John Holdrich, then Robert Felmingham. She obviously preferred her first husband: in her will of 1522 she asked to be buried beside him in Norwich Blackfriars. She gave eight pence to each friar there and four pence to each novice as well as money to repair the buildings. She described in detail the wall monument she wanted in the church there. It was to be of *latten* (brass or tin-plate) and the central portion was to be an image of the Blessed Virgin. To one side was to be her husband kneeling, with their two sons, one in his winding sheet, the other in armour. To the other side was Elizabeth kneeling, with three daughters all in winding sheets. (The children shown in winding sheets must have predeceased their mother). Unfortunately the monument has disappeared.

A final class of person buried in the cemeteries of monastic houses were of course the inhabitants themselves. Most were buried in the cemetery, the more important such as the abbot and priors might receive burial in the chapter house or in the church itself. Two stone coffins can still be seen in Wymondham abbey, presumably those of deceased priors.

Very few of these monastic burial monuments survive as most were destroyed with the churches themselves at the Dissolution. C. J. Palmer quotes an unnamed writer on the destruction at Gorleston friary: - *'the sacred building is gutted, and the labourers are now sacrilegiously pulling up the pavement; - a most sad spectacle! to see skulls, legs, arms and other bones of the dead lie about as though it were a bone house or a dog kennel'*. Even where the churches have survived, as at Norwich Cathedral and Wymondham,

How they lived - income and expenditure 111

there are few medieval monuments. The Cathedral has two tombs of members of the gentry of Norfolk who chose burial there: Sir James Hobart and Sir Thomas Windham. It also has chantry chapels for one prior, Simon Bozoun, and one bishop, James Goldwell. The latter still has embedded in it a musket ball from the days when the Parliamentary army was housed in the Cathedral in the late 1640s. Wymondham has a fine sixteenth century tomb of terracotta, traditionally said to be of Elisha Ferrers, the last abbot. Pevsner doubts this, however, on the grounds that it is stylistically too early, being very similar to tombs of the 1520s at Oxborough: Ferrers died in 1548.

52. A pilgrim emerges from a shell (a common badge of pilgrimage). From a Norwich Cathedral priory misericord (NRO, MC 186/82)

A few monastic monuments do survive in parish churches, having migrated over the centuries. The parish church of St Mary in South Walsham now houses the slab of the tomb of Richard of South Walsham, abbot of St Benet's, who died in 1439 and was buried at the abbey. After the Dissolution, the stone was taken from the abbey - at one time it was used as flooring in the Duke of Norfolk's palace in Norwich, and later as part of a sham ruin in Bracondale. It was brought to South Walsham church in the 1940s. The brass to Geoffrey of Langley, abbot of Horsham St Faith, was for a long time in the church of St Lawrence in Norwich: part of it is now in Horsham St Faith parish church. Halvergate parish church has a brass to Brother William, a Yarmouth Franciscan friar, who died in about 1440. This brass is a palimpsest - it has been turned over and reused. As the lady to whom the back is inscribed died in about 1540, the brass must have been reused a very short time after the Franciscan friary in Yarmouth was dissolved.

Ingham has a series of brasses of the Stapledon family, but that of Sir Miles the founder of the priory there, has disappeared: there was also a brass to a family dog, Jakke. The tomb of Sir Oliver de Ingham in the monastic chancel here is a fine one and captures something of the flavour of a military order: he wears full armour and appears contorted in agony. However although Sir Oliver built the chancel here (which is why he was buried in it) it was not until 15 years after his death that the priory was founded by his son-in-law. Another tomb in Ingham church also reminds us of the violence of medieval life. A knight, Sir Roger de Bois, appears to lie peacefully beside his wife Margaret. However, whereas her head rests on delicately carved pillows, his rests on the helmeted head of a decapitated victim.

A small part of the church of the Yarmouth Grey Friars survives. This includes two fourteenth century wall-tombs which both have paintings: these are the only wall paintings to survive from any friary building in England.

INCOME - BEQUESTS

Many people who did not choose burial in a religious house left money in their wills to one or more monastery. Norfolk is extremely fortunate to have an enormous number of wills surviving from 1370 onwards from which people's religious feelings at the hour of death can be analysed. Unfortunately very few wills survive before 1370: those of men leaving bequests to Norwich friaries, have already been considered. An extremely detailed will made by Oliver Wyth, a rich Yarmouth merchant who died in 1291 survives among the Norwich Cathedral archives. It has many bequests to religious houses. He did make a few gifts to traditional monasteries, but the great bulk of his charity went to nuns and to friaries. He left money to Carrow - not surprisingly as two of his daughters were nuns there - and to other female religious houses. He left money to all the Yarmouth friaries (five marks to the Black Friars, three marks to the Carmelites and one mark to the Austin friars in Gorleston) but it was the Franciscan friary he really favoured. He wished to be buried there, left 40 marks to raise the height of the gable of the church, 20 marks for clothing for the poorest of the friars and £10 for his funeral. He also left the Franciscan friary 80 marks to provide annual services for his soul and those of his relatives for 20 years. He instructed his heirs to provide £6 a year to pay to priests to celebrate for his soul 'for ever'. A further 20 shillings a year was to be given to pay to feed the friars on the anniversaries of the death of Wyth and of his wife Margaret, and to provide for two wax candles on the great altar of the friary church.

How they lived - income and expenditure 113

53 Brass to Geoffrey Langley, prior of Horsham St Faith. This drawing was made while the brass was at Norwich St Lawrence church: the lower half is now in Horsham St Faith parish church (NRO, MC 1741/31)

Wyth also left money to all the Norwich friaries (five marks to the Grey Friars, two marks each to the Black Friars and the Carmelites, five shillings each to the Friars of the Sack and the Pied Friars. The Austin Friars had not yet reached Norwich when he made his will). He went even further than this, leaving money to all the Black Friars' houses in East Anglia and to Grey Friars' houses throughout Britain.

The monastic house at Ingham is here taken as an example to show how medieval piety is reflected in fifteenth and early sixteenth century wills. Between 1420 and 1540 a total of 84 people left wills in the Norwich Consistory Court with bequests to this house. The sums ranged from 12 pence to 20 marks (about £14) but the great majority were of £1 or less: the total given over the 120 year period comes to rather less than £60. The testators came from 43 known parishes (in a few cases the parish is not given). As might be expected they are almost all in north east Norfolk, the only exceptions being Norwich itself, a group of three parishes in west Norfolk (Swaffham, Cockley Cley and Necton) and the parish of Covehithe in Suffolk. I have grouped these bequests into three 40-year bands to see if there is any change in the form of the bequests over time.

Between 1420 and 1460 a total of 14 people left money to Ingham. The sums varied from two shillings to 40 shillings. In addition one man left 6s.8d. to the prior and 3s.4d. to each canon. Two people left money to individually named canons. Two people, both in 1456, left bequests for the steeple: presumably it was being built at this date. No one left Ingham any land but two treasures were bequeathed to the canons there - a 'great piece of silver plate with a cover' and 'a large Agnus Dei of gold with relics to be hung up before the image of the Trinity there'. Three people asked to be buried in the church.

Between 1460 and 1500, 35 people left money to the house, again varying from two shillings to 40 shillings. Three left money specifically to the prior, five to all the canons and two made bequests to four individually named canons (one of whom was the testator's son). There was a bequest to the building of the steeple in 1483 - perhaps it was still not complete? Two people left money 'for grace and indulgence to my soul' and one man, a chaplain, left £6 to the guild of the Holy Trinity at Ingham. Only one person asked to be buried in the church in this period.

Between 1500 and 1540, 36 people left money to the house: these bequests continued into the 1530s with no obvious decline. The sums varied from 12 pence to five marks. Four bequests gave money to the prior and five to all the

How they lived - income and expenditure

canons, but no canons are mentioned by name. Two people asked to be buried in the church and one made his bequest partly dependent on permission being given: Philip Calthorpe (1514) offered 20 marks to the poor at Ingham and 10 marks to the house if he was buried there. If he was not (and he named his second choice as a burial place as Norwich White Friars) then Ingham was only to receive 20 shillings.

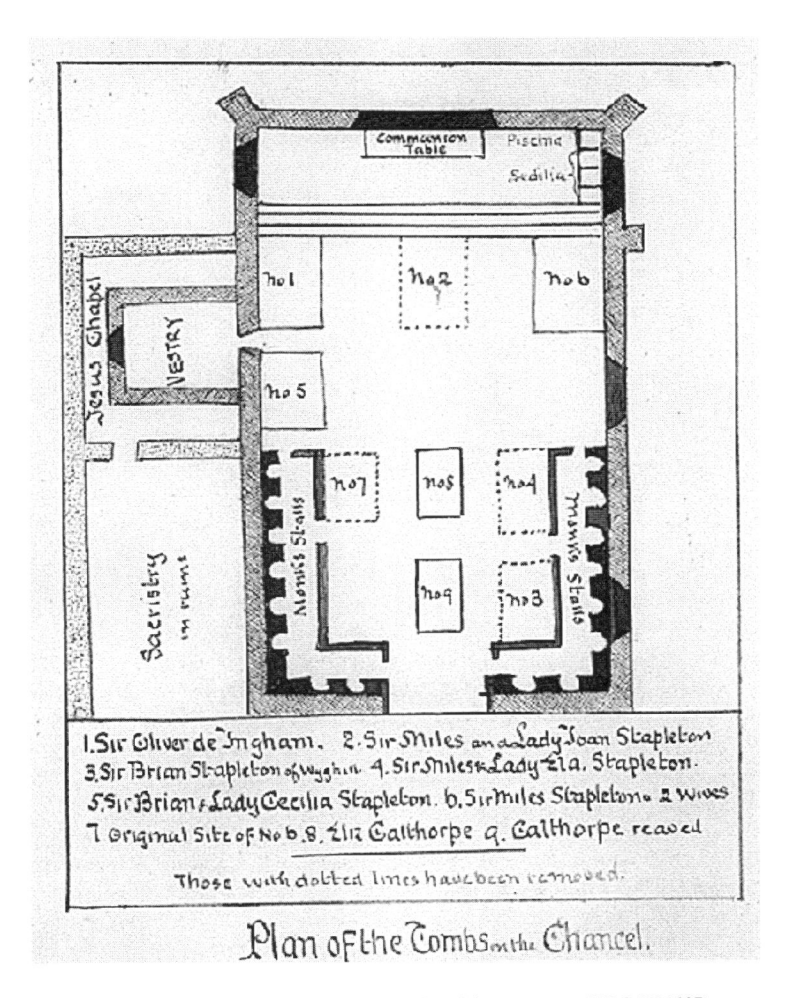

54. Ingham church, showing the monks' stalls and the monuments (MRO,RYE 137)

In the period 1500-1530 three people left land to the priory: no one had done this since 1420 (although several people had in the later fourteenth century when the priory was a relatively new foundation). Robert Smyth of Cockley Cley (1516) gave them 13 acres of land in Cockley Cley for 100 years. In return they were to keep a 'Mind Day' once a year for the souls of his parents, himself and his wife. This was to be held at St Peter's church, Cockley Cley, on the vigil of the feast day of St Peter in chains. After 100 years the land was to be sold and the money to be spent on a jewel for the use of the priory 'to remain there for ever in memory of him'. John Bardwell (1521) left them land in nearby Brumstead after the death of his wife Ann and William his son, to be held by the priory for 80 years if it could get a licence to acquire the land. If not, the land was to be sold and the money given to them to pray for the souls of John and his wife. The other testator to leave land was another local man, Robert Chubb, who bequeathed them five roods of land in Mill Hill, Ingham.

Similar bequests were made to Bromholme though some of the testators here were of higher status. Elizabeth Clere of the important Ormesby family (1446) left to every monk four pence as often as he should sing for her souls within 30 days of her death. Novices of course could not sing masses, but they too could help Elizabeth's soul into heaven: every novice saying 'Our Ladies' Psalter' received four pence, up to a limit of 33s. 4d. She left 20 shillings a year for two years to help her 'Year Day' for that term: a surprisingly modest request compared with Smyth's 100 years at Cockley Cley. She also left 33s. 4d. to repair buildings at Bromholme. The following year another high status benefactor, Lady Joan Bardolf, left the monastery a chalice.

At Bromholme, as at Ingham, bequests continued into the 1530s with no apparent falling-off. In 1531 Nicholas Carre, the Dean of St Mary in the Fields in Norwich left money to repair the east window of the priory church. In 1533 William Leiche left 3s. 4d. to the Holy Cross. In 1534 Richard Spanton made a will leaving 13s.4d. to the repair of the house, twelve pence to every monk being a priest and eight pence to every novice. The will was proved on Spanton's death in 1536: this was the very year that Bromholme was dissolved.

By the mid fourteenth century, however, people were tending to leave money to their parish churches rather than to monasteries, although the friars and the nuns were still favoured. Two examples from the wills among the Lynn borough archives illustrate this. In 1399 John Wace of Lynn left £30 to the church of St Nicholas and ten shillings to each of the other Lynn churches - St Margaret and St James. He left no money to any male religious house and

How they lived - income and expenditure 117

the - almost derisory - sum of eight pence to the four friaries in Lynn. However Wace clearly respected female religiosity: he left two marks to Blackborough and 20 shillings each to Marham, Crabhouse, Shouldham and to the nunnery in Cambridge. Thirty years later, Robert Salisbury made a similar range of bequests but he was clearly a fan of the friars as he left 6s. 8d. to each friary in Lynn and requested burial in that of the Franciscans. Salisbury also made no bequest to any male monastery, leaving money to the three Lynn churches and to Marham and Blackborough.

Despite the popularity of the friars, some people still did leave bequests to the monasteries, perhaps especially to local ones whose worth the testator knew from personal contact. For example, Peter Erl in 1440 took an interest in Mountjoy, which he referred to in his will as a 'poor monastery'. He gave them £20 but this was not to be given to them at once: they were to have £4 or five marks yearly 'for their clothing as long as it lasted'. (the money rather than the clothing!). John Anyngton of Thetford in his will of 1437 left money to the church of St Cuthbert, Thetford where he wished to be buried. He left money to the houses of monks, nuns and canons in Thetford but nothing to the two friaries in the town.

Although people could leave whatever sums of money they wanted to religious houses, standard fees for services naturally tended to develop. David Dymond estimates that in the early sixteenth century a commemorative mass at Thetford St Mary was costing about four pence. An anniversary obit - which involved the re-enactment of the funeral - was of course much more expensive, costing about 3s. 4d.

EXPENSES

The expenses of the monastic house were divided among the individual office-holders or *obedientiaries*. Each had their own income from particular estates so that there was normally no overall controller of the monastic budget. (There were exceptions: Marham had a bursar and at Old Buckenham there was an auditor - a layman - to look over the accounts.) If prayer was the key function of a monastery, then the key officials were the *sacrist* and the *precentor* who looked after the church and its services. The sacrist was responsible for supplies of wax (for candles), for incense and sacramental wine, and for maintaining the fixtures such as clocks. The precentor was responsible for the actual service, the music and the service books. The music was intended to be 'a source of delight and pleasure to God, the angels and mankind'. St Benet's had a master of obits specifically to organise the many masses said for the dead but in other houses this duty was that of the precentor.

Day to day life in the monastery is reflected in the names of other officials. The *cellarer* looked after the stores, the *refectorer* (or *fraterer*) the dining-room. Clothing was the responsibility of the *chamberlain*. As with most aspects of monastic life there was a move away from simplicity as the centuries passed. At Norwich Cathedral priory, for example, the monks' robes were originally made on site using wool from the sheep raised on the monastic estates. Later generations found it easier to buy their robes from suppliers in Norwich. Fashion occasionally entered even the monastic world - in 1532 two canons at Buckenham were rebuked for wearing pointed shoes. The various colours of robes worn were of course achieved by dyeing: the white robes of the Cistercian monks and white canons were simply undyed wool. They adapted them partly as being more simple and partly in tribute to the piety of the Blessed Virgin.

EXPENSES - HOSPITALITY

Two of the most visible officials to the outside world would be the *hostilar* and the *almoner*. The monastery was not supposed to turn anyone away, and was not to charge for its hospitality. This could be a considerable drain on the resources of the house. The guests were divided according to their status: rich and important people lodged with the abbot or prior, medium people in the monastic guest-house, poor people in the almoner's quarters. The retinues of noble guests could be enormous - when the Duke and Duchess of Clarence stayed at Lynn Austin friary they had 300 horses with them. An important house like this would also receive occasional royal guests: Edward I, II, III and Henry VII all stayed here with their retinue. They might leave a gift, of course, such as a jewelled cross or a gold cup. However when King John stayed for 13 days at Bury St Edmunds with all his retinue he contributed a mere 13 pence. Thetford Cluniac priory was crippled in 1279 by the brother of its patron, the Earl Marshall, who lived at the house and cost it more that all the monks put together. When Henry VII visited Thetford in 1498-9 he also stayed at the Cluniac priory: pewter borrowed from the beer-brewer for the occasion 'walked' with the royal party and had to be replaced at a cost to the monks of six shillings.

Important visitors had to be given presents as well. When Edward II visited the Norwich Dominican friary in 1326, the friars lined up and each one presented the king with an apple. Most gifts would be more substantial: When Henry VII and his retinue stayed at Lynn Austin friary in 1498, the friars' presents to him included ten pike and other fish, twelve swans, two oxen, twenty sheep and a tun of wine. In 1343 Norwich Cathedral priory noted the strain on its resources in the previous eight years caused by four visits from the king and three from the queen.

How they lived - income and expenditure 119

Some houses had so many visitors that they ran inns outside the precinct. Walsingham priory had several inns for the thousands of pilgrim visitors. The *Green Dragon* at Wymondham may have originated as a hostelry for visitors to the abbey as did the Swan adjoining the site of the west range of the cloister of Ingham priory. Thetford Cluniac priory owned the Angel Inn in the centre of town. Two lodges outside the gates at Bromholme are probably pilgrimage houses: they are of identical design, both resting on six brick piers. Bromholme also had an inn in Norwich, on All Saints Green. It was called The *Holy Rood of Bromholme* and must have been a popular resting place for pilgrims on their way to see the True Cross.

Monastic houses were also places of residence of various groups of people, from travellers taking advantage of their obligation of hospitality to people using the houses as places of retreat for a much longer period of time. Many ladies who stayed at Carrow brought their retinue, including male servants and chaplains with them. These would have lodged outside the cloister to secure the isolation of the nuns. Visitors might stay for other reasons: the Paston letters tell us that when Margery Paston fell in love with the family bailiff, Richard Calle, the family disapproved because of the class gulf. Both were lodged at Blackborough nunnery until the family reconciled themselves to the wedding. The son of this marriage, William Calle, became a Franciscan friar when he grew up: he was prior of the Norwich house at the time of the Dissolution.

The most famous resident of Carrow is perhaps Philip the Sparrow who was there with his owner Lady Jane Scrope when he was eaten by Gyb the monastery cat! The story was immortalised in verse by the local sixteenth century poet John Skelton:

Pla   ce   bo
Who is there, who?

Di   le   xi
Dame Margery,
Fa, re, my, my,
Wherefore and why, why?

For the sowle of Philip Sparowe
That was late slayn at Carowe
Among the Nones Blacke.

Although this may appear nonsense, it is in fact a subtle play on the service for the dead. 'Placebo' is the opening word of the service and 'Dilexi' that of the opening psalm. The spacing is intended to portray the plainsong chanting of the nuns. 'Fa, re my, my' represents the musical notes that mark the end of the Placebo.

One special class of long-term visitor to a monastic house was the corrodian. This was a person whom the monastery was bound to feed, and usually to house as well. They might be put into the house by the patron or by the royal family, usually as a form of 'retirement home'. For example in 1317 Langley was ordered to take in Robert de Maners who had served the king in Scotland but was now infirm. They were to maintain him for the rest of his life. The patronage of Creake was assigned to the Crown in 1231. This had a down side - the king could, and did, make the house look after royal servants who had been incapacitated. Other corrodians were individuals who paid a lump sum for being looked after for the rest of their lives. This was basically a gamble by the monastic house: whether there was a profit would depend on how long the individual lived. An example was that of Peter Nobys, master of Corpus Christi, Cambridge. He paid Thetford Cluniac priory £87 in the 1520s. In return he was to have a study and bedchamber over the sacristy, a stable for two horses, an annuity of five marks, freedom to walk in the monastic gardens, and a requiem mass after his death. He moved in, together with a personal servant. Nobys died only five years later, so presumably the house made a profit out of this corrody.

A dispute at the same house in 1315 reveals interesting details about the diet of the corrodians and the monks themselves. Two men complained that the prior refused to give them the daily allowance to which they were entitled. This was: a white loaf, a whole-meal loaf, a gallon and a half of the best beer, a portion of soup, a dish of meat on meat days from both courses - as much as the prior or two monks had. On the fish-days they were to have two courses of fish - if herrings they should have six herrings. If eggs were served they should have six eggs. For the second course they should receive as much as the prior did.

EXPENSES - EDUCATION

Another necessary expense was on education. In early years children would be brought to a monastery to be educated: some might then stay on to become monks or nuns. By the thirteenth century these schools had died out. Monks were to have a year's probation at the minimum age of 18 and to take the vows once the year was up. The minimum age of entry to an Austin friary

How they lived - income and expenditure 121

was 14 years, but was reduced to 11 years due to a shortage of numbers after the Black Death - however this younger age but was not adopted in all houses. It was clearly felt that this was too young an age for a lifelong commitment as is shown by two cases at Norfolk friaries. In 1402 William Heydok claimed he had made his vows at the age of only 11. One hundred years later Nicholas Hyndry supposedly made vows when he was under 13.

We know of these cases because they reached the Bishop's court. Both men were allowed to renounce their vows and so they ceased to be friars: however both appear to have chosen to remain parish priests.

55. Schoolmaster spanking a pupil. From a Norwich Cathedral priory misericord (NRO, MC 186/82)

All monasteries educated their novices and some taught poor boys in their almonry - Norwich Cathedral priory, for example, ran an elementary school. Some of the children did pay fees but children from poor families received free education. A schoolhouse is mentioned at Bromehill in 1514 - as there were only four monks and no novices here, this must have been for the village children. Many children stayed at monasteries and were presumably receiving some sort of education. Children staying at Carrow included some from the upper crust of Norfolk life - such as the niece of Bishop William Bateman and members of the Fastolf family. However merchants of Norwich sent their daughters to the priory too.

EXPENSES - CHARITY

Monasteries, as we have seen, were bound to give hospitality to all travellers, poor as well as rich. They also gave money or bread to the poor at their gates: the left-overs from the monastic table were supposed to be distributed to the poor, although in several cases there were complaints that the dogs were getting this surplus food first! Norwich Cathedral priory gave 10,000 loaves a year to their poor at their gate, and also provided food for prisoners in the Castle gaol, lepers, anchorites and other needy cases. The Cathedral sacrist gave money to the lepers in St Mary Magdalen hospital (the leper house on Sprowston road, now used as a library). He also provided cloth and shoes for the poor in the city.

Putting all sources together the Cathedral priory spent rather less than 10% of its income on charity. This compares favourably with the other house of which we have a detailed record, Thetford Cluniac priory. In 1539 they claimed they were spending over £32 a year on charity, but this was a lie, presumably designed to increase their chances of avoiding dissolution. David Dymond has analysed their register for the Norfolk Record Society: they gave ten shillings to the poor on Maundy Thursday. Apart from this their charity consisted of giving small sums of a few pence to individuals as the need arose: soldiers, prisoners, victims of fire and other such deserving cases. The whole came to about £10 a year, or roughly 2½% of the gross income of the house

Some houses maintained hospitals as part of their charitable work. Norwich Cathedral priory administered the hospital of St Paul in Norwich - this was the first hospital for the sick poor in the city and may well have been set up to relieve the burden on the almoner at the Cathedral priory. It provided for 20 permanent residents but also for any traveller in need of alms. They were looked after by 'sisters'. These were not, of course, qualified nurses but single women or widows themselves in need of charity. However some of them, at least, educated the poor children in their care. In 1558 a London priest called Thomas Salter left money to the hospital because he remembered that 72 years earlier one of the sisters, Katherine Peckham, was 'the first creature that taught me to know the letters in my booke'. This type of informal education no doubt took place at almost all the religious houses described in this book.

As we have seen, several houses of black canons began as hospitals. The priory at Massingham was originally termed a hospital and it continued to be seen in this light: in 1395 John Wilton, who had contracted leprosy while in the king's service was sent there to be cared for. However, in most cases the hospital side of the responsibilities of the monastic house was probably soon forgotten. Although Wormegay is described as having been set up for the care

How they lived - income and expenditure 123

of lepers in a royal confirmation of 1175, they are not mentioned in a grant to the house made twenty-five years later. The evidence in the caseof Creake is ambiguous: there is a reference to it as a hospital in 1397 but this could refer just to the hospital or infirmary for the canons there. Medieval hospitals were of course hospices for the dying rather than places where operations were conducted to cure people: the distinction between a hospital and a priory offering hospitality was not a clear-cut one.

Other monastic houses had similar responsibilities. In 1348, the canons of the Holy Sepulchre in Thetford were given the estates of the small hospital in the town known as Domus Dei. In return they were to maintain three poor people for forty weeks a year: every night they were each to be given a loaf of rye bread and a herring. If herring was not available they were to have two eggs instead. The Austin friary at Thetford maintained a small house for lepers in the former church of St John in Thetford, given to it by its founder. St Benet's ran the small hospital of St James in nearby Horning: the building survives as a barn of Horning Hall.

The poor might also benefit directly from a funeral at a monastic house. In 1494 Sir William Calthorpe requested burial in the Norwich Carmelite friary. He left 40 marks in pennies for poor people to pray for his soul - 'and more if need be'. In 1291 Oliver Wyth left the enormous sum of £84 to be distributed among the Yarmouth poor, on the day of his burial at the Franciscan friary, and on two later occasions - a week later and 30 days later. He also left money for later doles. Similar funerals took place in non-monastic churches of course: Baldwin Dereham, mentioned earlier, left a penny to every man, woman and child who attended his funeral in Crimplesham parish church.

Monasteries would also have a responsibility to the poor on their manors and in the parishes whose churches they owned. Creake Abbey was supposed to find a canon to celebrate mass in the chapel of St Thomas the Martyr every day and also to support five paupers there. They were to be given a loaf, broth, beer and a portion of meat or fish every day and also to be allowed a tunic every other year. However in 1341 it was alleged none of this had happened for at least two years. Others were more aware of their obligations: in a typical year (1301) the sacrist of Norwich Cathedral priory was giving over £4 to the poor of 'his' parishes at Scratby, Hemsby, Bawburgh and Eaton. Rather touchingly, the prior of the cell at Great Yarmouth treated the poor of the town (of whom there must have been many) to a dinner on each Christmas Day.

56. The prior's hall, Great Yarmouth Benedictine priory: this photograph was taken in the 1860s, after the building had become a school (NRO, Y/YTC 86/12/64)

THE END

Monasticism in England came to a sudden end in the years between 1536 and 1540 when all monasteries were compulsorily dissolved by Henry VIII or 'voluntarily' surrendered to him. However several groups of monasteries had disappeared in earlier centuries.

There was always a danger of smaller houses simply running out of occupants. Some were no more than cells of larger monasteries, and in some cases it is not even clear whether they were formal cells or just gathering-points for estate revenues. At Modney there may have been just a prior and a monk acting as estate manager. The house at Sheringham was a cell of Notley. There were only two or three canons here, and even these did not come after about 1345. Even the cells of Norwich Cathedral priory had only a few monks in residence, perhaps half a dozen at Yarmouth and Lynn and just two or three at Aldeby and St Leonard's.

Smaller monasteries might have to give up the struggle for independence and become cells of larger houses. At Molycourt there was only one monk after the prior died in 1390. The solitary monk, Stephen Wyse, became prior himself but the cause was a lost one: Molycourt became a cell of Ely in 1446. Wormegay became a cell of Pentney in 1468 and Massingham a cell of Castle Acre in 1475. Peterstone was said in 1416 to be in a poor way because of the plague of 1349 and flood in 1378 and 1387. Some time later it was made a cell of Walsingham. Other houses just faded away. Guthlac's Stowe is one such: the last known documentary reference to the monastery is in 1464.

Some houses came to a sudden end as a result of a disaster. The house at Creake was wiped out in 1506 when all the canons died of plague within a week. Its property passed automatically to the Crown and was granted to Christ's College, Cambridge. There must have been rumours of buried treasure on the site: in 1528 a monk from St Benet's came to the deserted abbey with a necromancer called John Sharpe 'who called to the spirit of the treasure'. However they found nothing. The Carmelite friary in Yarmouth burnt down in 1509 and the Dominican one in 1525: it does not appear that either was rebuilt. In 1557 that part of Yarmouth Town Wall near the former Black Friars fell down. It was rebuilt using some of the stones of the friary: the white limestone blocks can still be seen in the wall of flint.

57. Creake abbey in the mid-nineteenth century (NRO, MS 4576)

One group of monastic houses to disappear early was that known as the alien priories. These were dependent on parent houses in France to whom they contributed funds. They included all the Cluniac houses: as we have seen these were all dependencies of Cluny itself. The idea of English money going to France was naturally unpopular, especially during the many periods that the two countries were at war: in 1307 English Cluniac houses were ordered to stop sending money to the abbot of Cluny. Alien priories were always liable to fines and confiscations and two Norfolk houses - Witchingham and Well Hall priory in Gayton - were taken over by the Crown in the reign of Edward III. It was possible for some monastic houses (usually the larger ones) to escape dissolution by paying a fine for a declaration that they were no longer alien but denizen, that is English: Horsham St Faith did this in 1390 and Castle Acre Cluniac priory in 1373. The small house of St Winwaloy escaped confiscation by becoming a cell of West Dereham in the early fourteenth century.

The end

In 1414 an Act was passed suppressing all the remaining alien priories. Norfolk ones included Docking, Field Dalling, Horstead, Sporle, Toft Monks and Lessingham. Estates owned by French monasteries were also confiscated, including land at West Wretham owned by the abbey of Conques. These resources passed to the Crown: most was eventually used for educational or charitable purposes. For example, the estates of Sporle were given to Eton College and those of Toft Monks to King's College, Cambridge. The Field Dalling property remained in monastic hands, being granted successively to several religious institutions and eventually to the Carthusian priory at Mount Grace in Yorkshire. They did not establish a cell however, merely farming it as an estate.

The final dress rehearsal for Dissolution was when Cardinal Wolsey closed a number of small houses to use their revenues to fund colleges at Cambridge and Ipswich. This was done under papal bulls of 1518 and 1524 but many of the intended houses escaped because of Wolsey's sudden fall in 1528 with the project still incomplete. In Norfolk, Bromehill was dissolved under Wolsey, but the proposed closures at Wendling and Mountjoy were not carried out. The monks, canons and nuns were given a choice of moving to another monastic house (chosen for them by Cardinal Wolsey) or of returning to the world with a payment of about £1 each but without any pension. One nun is known to have moved to Thetford nunnery from Wise, Essex, when the latter house was closed down.

In 1535 Thomas Cromwell became Vicar-General. He was responsible for the *Valor Ecclesiasticus*, which assessed the wealth held by the church and whose valuations of monastic houses have already been used several times in this book. The two richest monasteries in Norfolk by far were Walsingham priory and Norwich Cathedral priory, both valued at over £700 a year. The values given in *Valor Ecclesiasticus* are very important for assessing the *relative* wealth of monastic houses. (The figures in themselves mean relatively little to us today both because of the vast change in the value of the pound and because of uncertainties in exactly how the calculations of value were made). The figures are not complete - the friaries were not included and about five other houses escaped valuation for various reasons. Of the 37 Norfolk houses that were valued, 22 were worth less than £100 a year (including all five nunneries) and eight at between £100 and £199 (including the double house at Shouldham). The poorest houses of all were Slevesholm valued at a mere £1 a year and Modney at £2: however these were effectively just cells of the much larger houses at Ely and Ramsey respectively. The poorest of the independent houses was Weybridge, valued at £7 a year.

The seven houses in Norfolk worth more that £200 a year were:

Norwich Cathedral priory	£874
Walsingham priory	£791
St Benet's abbey	£583
Castle Acre priory	£306
Thetford Cluniac priory	£312
Westacre priory	£266
Wymondham abbey	£211

Cromwell also carried out a general visitation of the monastic houses, and also of the friaries. These asked 86 questions (12 of which were addressed to nunneries only) of the kind that bishops were accustomed to ask when they visited monastic houses. They were about how the services were conducted, the state of the buildings, how the novices were trained etc. Like the bishops they then issued injunctions tightening things up - for example by forbidding monks to leave the monastic precinct, or insisting that alms were given according to the terms of the foundation charter, or that left-overs from monastic meals really went to the poor.

These proceedings were followed by the Act of 1536, which formally dissolved all small monasteries. The original plan was to close down every house with fewer than twelve inhabitants. This was later changed to a financial barrier: those worth less than £200 a year were to be closed. The Act talks about 'manifest sin, vicious, carnal and abominable living daily used and committed among the little and small abbeys'. In contrast, it says, the large houses were well kept and observed religion. Moral conduct can, of course, never be defined as simply as this. The real point of closing the monasteries was a simple one: all their property was taken over by the Crown. The king was then free to dispose of it as he wished. Sales of former monastic lands gave an enormous boost to royal revenues.

Inhabitants of the 200 houses closed in 1536 could either move into the large houses or take 'capacities' - that is be given dispensation to serve as secular clergymen. Heads of houses were given generous pensions but the others were not. However they did receive arrears of wages and a 'reward' or lump sum payment. Most seem to have decided to take the dispensations, as did every canon at Westacre for example. Some became parish priests (many of the canons already were, of course), others found work as chantry priests. There were 30 houses in Norfolk valued at less than £200 a year but as the cells were counted in with their parent houses they were not dissolved. The number of Norfolk houses dissolved as a result of the 1536 Act was actually 22, with a total value of £1,583.

All five female religious houses were dissolved in 1536 (but not the twin house at Shouldham). As with the monks, the heads of these houses received a reward and a pension, the nuns a reward only. The pensions given were roughly in proportion to the value of the house, ranging from £8 a year to Cecily Suffield, prioress of Carrow, down to £4 a year to Elizabeth Studfield, prioress of Crabhouse. The rewards given to the nuns varied from 20 shillings to 45 shillings. Nuns of course could not become priests: they had the choice of moving to another nunnery or of taking their reward and moving into secular life. Of the nuns in the five houses only eight chose to be transferred to other nunneries - four from Carrow, one from Crabhouse and three from Marham. Shouldham was saved in 1536 because all the Gilbertine houses escaped dissolution after a personal intervention to the king by their ex-master, Dr Holgate, who was Bishop of Llandaff.

A total of 200 monasteries and 50 nunneries survived the dissolution under the Act of 1536. By 1540 they were all gone. Although this seems like step-by-step planning by Henry VIII and Cromwell, this was not in fact the case. Henry actually founded two new monastic houses after the Act, at Stixwould in 1536 and Bisham in 1537. Although they proved to have very short lives, their existence shows that the king was not yet committed to total abolition.

The larger monasteries were not all closed down under further legislation: basically most were bullied into voluntary surrender. As people saw what was happening, gifts to friaries and monasteries dried up. They were forced to sell their assets - Norwich Dominican priory sold one of their bells to the parish church of St Andrew just across the road. The canons of Westacre saw the end too and sold off much of their property, tying the title deeds up with such legal complexity that the land could not be recovered when the house was finally dissolved. The prior made £489 for himself from these sales and the canons shared out a much smaller amount. Many others saw the inevitable and made arrangements of their own. There was only one canon left at Thetford St Sepulchre in 1536, although there were still 16 servants. The Commissioners reported *'there is no earthly thing here at all but trash and baggage'*. When the Commissioners arrived at Ingham in 1536 all the canons had already gone. The two remaining canons at Weybourne also appear to have sold off most of the moveable goods before the Royal Commissioners visited the house.

Voluntary surrenders continued throughout 1537 and 1538. Castle Acre surrendered with its parent house, Lewes, in November 1537, Wymondham and Walsingham in the following year. The previous year a group of people dared to petition the king to preserve Walsingham. This so-called

'Walsingham rebellion' led to the execution of eleven of the ringleaders in Norwich, Yarmouth and Lynn as well as at Walsingham itself, where the sub-prior Nicholas Mileham was one of two men to be hung, drawn and quartered outside the priory gates. This act of excessive violence must have served as a grim warning to the other monastic houses and those who supported them. However this was the only act of violence connected with the Dissolution in the county - although Edmund Harcocke, the prior at Norwich Blackfriars, was lucky to escape unpunished for a sermon critical of the royal supremacy that he preached in 1535 and which attracted the attention of Thomas Cromwell himself. The last Norfolk house to close was that of Carbrooke, dissolved together with all the houses of the Hospitallers on 7 May 1540.

The closure of the monasteries was described in dramatic terms by Hook: *'As the inmates went out by one door, those employed to dismantle the house, either for the king or for those whom the property had already been sold, entered by another ... The stalls where the monks had prayed were rudely torn down: the painted windows were demolished: the shrines were rifled; the tombs thrown open. From the stones the brasses were rent; from the skeletons, gold and jewels were torn. The rudeness of an hour annihilated the pious labour of ages; barbarians triumphed over superstition'*.

Norwich Cathedral priory was dissolved as a monastic house but continued as a cathedral - technically it was 'changed'. Norwich was the first of the Cathedral priories to be dissolved, on 2 May 1538. The priory was replaced with a dean and chapter. However as the prior became dean, the senior monks prebendaries and almost all other monks minor canons the change was not so very great. They merely threw off their monks' robes and took on those of secular clergymen. Although the monastic library was dispersed, the working archives of the Cathedral priory survived because of this continuity: they include one of the richest series of account rolls from any monastery in Britain.

Just one monastery in England technically escaped dissolution, that of St Benet's. This was because in 1535 it had been united to the bishopric of Norwich who took over its revenues (and gave his former revenues to the king in exchange). The Bishop of Norwich thus became the abbot of St Benet's and continued to be summoned to the House of Lords under this title: this is why he holds the yearly service at St Benet's mentioned earlier. However there were no monks there after the early 1540s. Most of the buildings including the church were pulled down by Bishop Parkhurst in the 1560s and 1570s. The abbot's house survived and was a public house in the nineteenth century: it burnt down towards the end of the century and nothing remains of it. The gatehouse also survived and was converted into a windmill

The end

58. Dramatic view of St Benet's abbey gatehouse, showing the cap to the windmill, which has since disappeared. (NRO, from MC 186/84)

in the early eighteenth century: this forms one of the most striking features of the Broadland landscape even today.

In one important way the king was more generous than when earlier houses had been dissolved: pensions were granted not only to the heads of the houses but also to all the other inhabitants as well. Because the surrenders were the result of individual negotiation the amount of the pension varied from house to house. Rates to heads of houses were generous, even to those who had committed recent misdemeanours: the prior of Westacre, William Wingfield, received £40 a year and the prior of Walsingham £100 a year.

Average pensions for ordinary monks and canons were about £6 a year in the Norwich diocese, rather higher than the national average of £5 a year. However this was only an average: those from the smaller houses might receive less. The two canons left at Weybourne had taken it in turn to be prior, John Frost between 1526 and 1530 and John Bulman from 1530 onwards. Bulman was the luckier: as prior at the Dissolution he received a pension of £4 a year. Frost was only granted £3 a year, well below a living wage. Many of the men of course could find jobs as parish priests, especially if lay patrons were generous: by 1541 nine former monks of Thetford Cluniac priory had been given parish livings by the Duke of Norfolk. John Bulman became rector of Egmere in 1543 so he had to live on his pension for only six years. So many former monks, canons and friars were becoming parish priests that in many dioceses there were almost no ordinations of new priests in the 1540s and early 1550s.

As always, the females received less generous treatment. Pensions granted to nuns averaged about £3 a year. Obviously they could not find work as priests and many returned to their families - two Norfolk nuns at Barking, Margerie Paston and Gabrielle Shelton, returned to their family houses in the county when the nunnery was dissolved. Ironically Gabrielle's new family home was at Carrow, no longer a nunnery but now a private house which her father, Sir John Shelton, had bought from the Crown. When the double house at Shouldham was dissolved in 1538, the men inevitably got the better deal even though the house was designed primarily for nuns with the canons there to support them. The male prior received a pension of £20 a year, the head of the female house only £5 a year. The canons each received 54s. 4d. a year, the nuns between 13s.4d. and 40 shillings.

The arrangements for receiving the money were the same for the nuns as for the monks. The pensions were given out in two instalments each year at Norwich and Bury St Edmunds: the pensioners might have to travel quite a distance to receive their money.

There was less reason to abolish the friaries as they did not own the great tracts of land that the monasteries did. However their direct allegiance to the Pope was a threat to the king. The observant Franciscans were suppressed in 1534 because of their loyalty to the king's first wife, Katherine of Aragon. The other friaries were all dissolved in 1538 under a fiction that they were surrendering voluntarily because of poverty and debt. A story about the Norwich Carmelite friary illustrates the uncertainty and violence of the times. A man called John Pratt called on the friary while the friars were at dinner and demanded to see the prior. He claimed that he was a servant of Thomas Cromwell and that he had a commission on him to suppress the house. He obviously hoped the prior would pay him to go away. Instead the prior had Pratt hauled before the Mayor's Court. Here Pratt confessed to fraud. His sentence was to be nailed by his ears to the pillory in Norwich Market Place. When the time came for his release his ears were simply lopped off.

Friars did not receive pensions but those who took their surrender were bound to make some provision for them. A few probably went abroad to continue the religious life but most became parish or chantry clergymen like the monks and canons. A royal decree of 1546 finally suppressed all four orders of friars.

This is not the place to describe the subsequent history of the English church. There was a major change to the lives of clergymen - including many former monks and friars - under Edward VI when for the first time they were allowed to take wives. When his sister Mary came to the throne in 1553 she forbade clergy to be married: nearly 100 former religious in Norwich diocese were deprived of their livings because they had married. Mary made John Hopton, a former Dominican friar, Bishop of Norwich. He was responsible for the burning of 48 people in the diocese for 'heresy', most at Lollards' Pit in Norwich. Mary also tried to re-establish monasticism but this was strongly opposed by the gentlemen of England, many of whom profited from owning ex-monastic land of course. Mary's reign was a short one. With the accession of her sister Elizabeth in 1558 the Reformation - and the dissolution of the monasteries - was assured. Recent work by Muriel McClendon suggests in Norwich at least the magistrates were remarkably tolerant of people's expression of their religious opinions in this period - for example only two of the people burnt in Norwich were actually from the city, and even these had chosen to defy authority by making public statements of their views.

Were the monastic houses missed? The answer depends in the end upon one's own faith. As we have stressed the principal role of a religious house was to offer up prayer. Belief in the power of intercessory prayer tended to be replaced by belief in individual prayer in the later Middle Ages, so the need for monasteries was no longer so great. By the fifteenth century people tended to be leaving money for their own parish church rather than to monastic houses: the later abolition of gilds and chantries based on parish churches may well have had a more direct effect on people's lives than the abolition of the monasteries. Pilgrimage, too, had lost its meaning for some people. The Lollards, for example, condemned it as useless: a defendant at the Norwich heresy trials in the fifteenth century pointedly referred to 'Our Lady of *Falsingham*'. However the more active role of the friars in town life and the nuns in village life was still appreciated: bequests to these houses continued right down until the Dissolution.

The charitable work of monastic houses was also missed. We have seen that a relatively small percentage of income was devoted to almsgiving - perhaps 5% or so. However we have also seen that this income came from an

59. The remains of Hickling priory, now a farm (NRO, MC 530/2)

enormous quantity of land - perhaps a quarter of the land in England. Even 5% of this income from such vast estates amounted to a very considerable sum. When the monasteries were dissolved the land passed to the Crown and then to individual landlords: they certainly did not give 5% - or in most cases anything at all - to the poor. This created a crisis: as early as the 1540s the authorities in Norwich were being swamped by the problem of what to do with their poor people. As the town clerk of Norwich graphically wrote over a century after the dissolution of the monasteries - 'poverty daily invades us like an armed man'. The Tudor authorities realised the gap that had been created and eventually legislated to make each parish responsible for its own poor. For the previous 500 years it had been the charity of the monastic community that had looked after the poor, concerning themselves with both their physical and their spiritual welfare. Now they were gone and there was no one to care.

The power of monastic sites over the imagination is perhaps reflected in the number of ghost stories centred around them. Norfolk has its share. The beach at Bacton is haunted by a monk from nearby Bromholme. He was walking there when a girl was washed up in a storm. She died in his arms and the monk died too, of a broken heart. St Benet's is haunted by a monk who betrayed the abbey to the Normans on condition that he was made abbot. The Normans did make him abbot but promptly hanged him at the monastery gate as a traitor: his shrieks can still be heard. (There is no evidence at all to back up this often-told story although chroniclers do disagree about the fate of the last Saxon abbot: William Worcester says that he fled to Denmark but Oxenedes says that he remained in office under the Normans.)

It was probably the superior quality of monastic drains that led to the story of an underground passage from Binham priory to Walsingham. Underground passages and ghosts both appear in the story of the mad monk of Hickling: he would emerge from either end of the passage, with parchment and quill, having been driven insane adding up the monastic accounts! The dancing monks seen at Ingham were supposedly disturbed when their bones were removed after the Dissolution. Within living memory, bones unearthed at Lyng were associated with the nunnery there: children were let off school early so they did not have to walk past the place where the bones were found after dark.

Whatever the truth of these stories, many of the Norfolk monastic sites retain an atmosphere conducive to spiritual contemplation half a millennium after the departure of the last monk. The powerful influence of centuries of communal prayer remains with us today.

60. W.H. Cooke's drawing of Ingham priory, complete with ghost
(NRO, MS 4311)

FURTHER READING

BASKERVILLE, G., *English Monks and the Suppression of the Monasteries* (1937).

BLOMEFIELD, F, *An essay towards a topographical history of Norfolk 1739-1775* (second edition 1805-1810).

BURTON, J., *Monastic and Religious Orders in Britain 1000-1300* (1994).

CROSSLEY, F. H., *The English Abbey* (1935).

DAVIS, R. H. C. A., *History of Medieval Europe* (1987 edition).

DICKINSON, J. C., *Monastic Life in Medieval Englan,* (1961).

FREEDBERG, D., *The Power of Images* (1989).

GILCHRIST, R., *Norwich Cathedral: A Biography of the North Transept,* (in JBAA cli 1998, 107-136).

GILCHRIST, R., and OLIVA, M., *Religious Women in Medieval East Anglia* (1993).

HANAWALT, B., *Crime in East Anglia in the Fourteenth Century* (Norfolk Record Society volume 44, 1976).

KNOWLES, D., *The Monastic Order in England* (1940).

KNOWLES, D., *The Religious Orders in England* (1948-59).

LASKO, P., and MORGAN, N. J., *Medieval Art in East Anglia 1300-1520* (1973).

MARTIN, T. A., *History of the town of Thetford* (1779)

McCLENDON, M., *The Quiet Reformation* (1999).

MEERES, F., *A History of Norwich* (1998).

OLIVA, M., *The Convent and the Community in Late Medieval England* (1998)

PALMER, C. J., *The Perlustration of Great Yarmouth* (1872-1875).

PEVSNER, N. and WILSON, B., *The Buildings of England - Norwich and North-East Norfolk* (1997).

PEVSNER, N. and WILSON, B., *The Buildings of England - North-West and South Norfolk* (1999).

RICHARDS, P., *King's Lynn* (1990).

RICHMOND, W. R., *The Story of Great Yarmouth* (undated).

RYE, W. A., *History of Norfolk* (1885).

SUTERMEISTER, H., *The Norwich Blackfriar*, (1977).

TANNER, N., *The Church in Late Medieval Norwich 1370-1552* (1984).

TAYLOR, R., *Index Monasticus* (1821).

THOMPSON, S., *Women Religious* (1991).

Victoria History of the County of Norfolk, volume 2 (1906).

YAXLEY, D., *The Prior's Manor Houses* (1988). A transcription of mid-fourteenth century inventories of manor houses of Norwich Cathedral priory.

The *Norfolk Record Society* has transcribed the following monastic material:

St Benet's cartulary (NRS volumes 2 and 3)

The first register of Norwich Cathedral priory (NRS volume 11)

The Norfolk section of the cartulary of Lewes priory (NRS volume 12)

Bromholme priory cellarer's roll, 1415-6 (NRS volume 17)

Creake abbey cartulary (NRS volume 35)

Norwich Cathedral priory communar's rolls (NRS volume 51)

Register of Thetford Cluniac priory, 1482-1540 (NRS volumes 59 and 60)

Norwich Cathedral priory gardener's rolls (NRS volume 61)

Norfolk Archaeology includes important articles on many of the monastic sites discussed in this book and transcriptions of some of the records.

GAZETEER OF NORFOLK MONASTIC HOUSES

NAME	PARISH	TYPE	DATES	REMAINS
ALDEBY PRIORY	Aldeby	Benedictine Monks (cell to Norwich)	c.1100 - 1538	E
BEESTON REGIS PRIORY	Beeston Regis	Black Canons	*temp.* John or Henry III - 1539	B
BINHAM PRIORY	Binham	Benedictine Monks	*temp.* Henry I - 1539	A
BLACKBOROUGH PRIORY	Middleton	Benedictine Nuns	c.1200 - 1537	D
BLAKENEY FRIARY	Blakeney	Carmelite Friars	c. 1295 - 1538	C
BROMEHILL PRIORY	Weeting	Black Canons	*temp.* John - 1528	D
BROMHOLME PRIORY	Bacton	Cluniac Monks (cell to Castle Acre until 1195)	1113 - 1536	B
BUCKENHAM PRIORY	Buckenham, Old	Black Canons	1146 - 1536	E
BURNHAM NORTON FRIARY	Burnham Norton	Carmelite Friary	c. 1241 - 1538	B
CARBROOKE, GREAT	Carbrooke	Commandery and Chapel of Knights Hospitallers	before 1173 - 1540	E
CARBROOKE, LITTLE	Carbrooke	Commandery of Sisters Hospitallers	*temp.* Henry II - c. 1180	E
CARROW PRIORY	Norwich, Carrow	Benedictine Nuns	1146 - 1536	B

139

CASTLE ACRE PRIORY	Castle Acre	Cluniac Monks (cell to Lewes until 1373)	1085 - 1537	A
CHOSELEY	Choseley	Preceptory of the Order of St Lazarus of Jerusalem (cell to Burton Lazars)	*temp.* Henry I - 1536	E
COXFORD PRIORY	East Rudham	Black Canons	*temp.* Stephen - 1536	C
CRABHOUSE PRIORY	Wiggenhall St Mary Magdalene	Austin Nuns	c. 1181 - 1537	E
CREAKE ABBEY	Creake, North	Black Canons	1206 - 1506	B
CUSTHORPE	Westacre	Black Canons (cell to Westacre)	*?temp.* William II - 1538	E
DEREHAM	Dereham, East or West	Saxon Nunnery	c. 645 - c.790	E
DEREHAM, WEST, ABBEY	Dereham, West	White Canons	c.1188 - 1536	D
DOCKING PRIORY	Docking	Alien (Ivry Benedictine monks)	c.1209 - 1414	E
FIELD DALLING PRIORY	Field Dalling	Alien Savigny (Cistercian monks)	1138-1414	E
FLITCHAM PRIORY	Flitcham	Black Canons (cell to Walsingham)	*?temp.* Henry III - 1538	D
GORLESTON AUSTIN FRIARS	Gorleston	Austin Friars	Before 1311 - 1538	D
GUTHLAC'S STOW	Swaffham	Cluniac Monks (cell to Castle Acre)	*temp* Henry II - after 1440	E

Gazeteer

HADDISCOE PRECEPTORY	Haddiscoe	Knights Templars	before 1218 - 1312	E
HEACHAM PRIORY	Heacham	Cluniac Monks (cell to Lewes)	*temp.* William II - 1537	E
HEMPTON PRIORY	Hempton	Black Canons	*temp.* Henry I - 1536	D
HICKLING PRIORY	Hickling	Black Canons	1185 - 1536	C
HORSHAM ST FAITH PRIORY	Horsham St Faith	Benedictine Monks Alien (Conques) until 1390	1105 - 1536	C
HORSTEAD PRIORY	Horstead	Alien (Caen Benedictine Monks)	*temp.* William II - 1414	E
INGHAM PRIORY	Ingham	Trinitarian Canons	c. 1360 - 1536	C
LANGLEY ABBEY	Langley	White Canons	1198 - 1536	C
LESSINGHAM PRIORY	Lessingham	Alien (Bec Benedictine Monks)	*temp.* William I - 1414	E
LYNG PRIORY	Lyng	Benedictine Nuns	date of foundation not known, moved to Thetford 1176	E
LYNN PRIORY	Lynn	Benedictine Monks	c. 1100 - 1538	C
LYNN - AUSTIN FRIARS	Lynn	Austin Friars	before 1293 - 1538	D
LYNN - BLACK FRIARS	Lynn	Dominican Friars	1272 - 1538	E
LYNN - FRIARS OF THE SACK	Lynn	Friars of the Sack	before 1276 - 1307	E

LYNN - GREY FRIARS	Lynn	Franciscan Friars	before 1264 - 1538	C
LYNN - WHITE FRIARS	Lynn	Carmelite Friars	1269 - 1538	D
MARHAM ABBEY	Marham	Cistercian Nuns	1249 - 1536	C
MASSINGHAM PRIORY	Massingham, Great	Black Canons	before 1260 -1538	D
MODNEY PRIORY	Hilgay	Benedictine Monks Alien (later cell to Ramsey)	before 1291 - 1538	E
MOLYCOURT PRIORY	Outwell	Saxon Benedictine Order, a cell of Ely from c.1445	date of foundation not known - 1538	E
MOUNTJOY PRIORY	Haveringland	Augustinian Canons	*temp.* Richard I or John -1536	E
NORMANSBURGH PRIORY	South Raynham	Cluniac Monks (cell to Castle Acre)	1160 - 1537	E
NORWICH - FRIARY OF OUR (?BLESSED) LADY	Norwich	Friars of Our (Blessed) Lady [could be two different small friaries]	before 1290 - ?1307	E
NORWICH - PIED FRIARS	Norwich	Pied Friars	date of foundation not known - 1307	E
NORWICH - AUSTIN FRIARS	Norwich	Austin Friars	1293 - 1538	D
NORWICH - BLACK FRIARS, 1st HOUSE	Norwich	Dominican Friars	1226 - 1538	E
NORWICH - BLACK FRIARS, 2nd HOUSE	Norwich	Dominican Friars	1307 - 1538	A
NORWICH - GREY FRIARS	Norwich	Franciscan Friars	1226 - 1538	D

NORWICH - FRIARS OF THE SACK	Norwich	Friars of the Sack	c.1250 - 1307	E
NORWICH - WHITE FRIARS	Norwich	Carmelite Friars	c.1256 - 1538	C
NORWICH - ST LEONARD'S PRIORY	Norwich, Thorpe	Benedictine Monks (cell to Norwich)	1096 - 1538	D
NORWICH CATHEDRAL PRIORY	Norwich	Benedictine Monks	1096 - 1538	A
PENTNEY PRIORY	Pentney	Black Canons	*temp*. William I - 1537	C
PETERSTONE PRIORY	Burnham Overy	Black Canons	date of foundation not known - 1449	D
PRIOR'S THORNS	Swaffham	Cistercian Monks (cell to Sawtry)	*temp.* Henry II - 1538	E
SHERINGHAM PRIORY	Sheringham	Black Canons (cell to Notley)	c.1162 - c. 1345	E
SHOULDHAM PRIORY	Shouldham	Gilbertine Canons and Nuns	*temp.* Richard I - 1539	E
SLEVESHOLM PRIORY	Methwold	Cluniac Monks (cell to Castle Acre)	*temp.* Stephen - 1537	E
SPORLE PRIORY	Sporle	Alien (Saumers Benedictine Monks)	? *temp.* Henry I - 1414	E
ST BENET'S OF HOLME ABBEY	Horning	Benedictine Monks	c. 800 - (1535)	B
ST WINWALOY'S PRIORY	Wereham	Alien (Mounstrol Benedictine Monks) Cell to West Dereham after 1336	Date of foundation not known - 1536.	E

THETFORD - ST GEORGE PRIORY	Thetford	Benedictine Nuns (formerly Benedictine monks)	Saxon priory from c. 1020; nunnery c.1176 (from Lyng)-1537	C
THETFORD ST MARY PRIORY	Thetford	Cluniac Monks (cell to Cluny until 1375)	1104 - 1540	A
THETFORD - PRIORY OF THE HOLY SEPULCHRE	Thetford	Canons of the Holy Sepulchre	1139 - 1536	C
THETFORD - AUSTIN FRIARS	Thetford	Austin Friars	1389 - 1538	E
THETFORD - BLACK FRIARS	Thetford	Dominican Friars	between 1325 and 1345 - 1538	E
TOFT MONKS PRIORY	Toft Monks	Alien (Preaux Benedictine Monks)	*temp.* Henry I - 1414	E
WALSINGHAM PRIORY	Walsingham, Little	Black Canons	1169 - 1538	A
WALSINGHAM - GREY FRIARS	Walsingham, Little	Franciscan Friars	c.1346 - 1538	B
WELL HALL PRIORY	Gayton	Alien (Caen Benedictine Monks)	c.1081 - 1339	E
WENDLING ABBEY	Wendling	White Canons	c.1267 - 1536	D
WESTACRE PRIORY	Westacre	Black Canons (cell to Lewes)	? *temp.* William II - 1538	C
WEYBOURNE PRIORY	Weybourne	Black Canons (cell to Westacre until 1314)	*temp.* John - 1536	B
WEYBRIDGE PRIORY	Acle	Black Canons	? *temp.* Edward I - 1536	D
WITCHINGHAM PRIORY	Great Witchingham	Alien (Longueville Cluniac Monks)	*temp.* William I - *temp.* Edward III	E

WORMEGAY PRIORY	Wormegay	Black Canons	Before 1175- 1537	E
WYMONDHAM PRIORY later ABBEY	Wymondham	Benedictine Monks (cell to St Albans until 1448)	1107 - 1537	A
YARMOUTH - BLACK FRIARS	Great Yarmouth	Dominican Friars	c. 1270 - 1538	E
YARMOUTH - GREY FRIARS	Great Yarmouth	Franciscan Friars	*temp.* Henry III - 1538	B
YARMOUTH PRIORY	Great Yarmouth	Benedictine Monks (cell to Norwich)	c.1100 - 1538	C
YARMOUTH - WHITE FRIARS	Great Yarmouth	Carmelite Friars	1278 - 1538	E

REMAINS

A	Worth a special visit
B	Worth a detour
C	Fragments or one large feature remains
D	Shapeless walls
E	No remains

IMPORTANT NOTE ALL BUILDINGS IN CATEGORY A AND SOME IN CATEGORY B ARE OPEN TO THE PUBLIC AT REASONABLE TIMES.

SOME BUILDINGS IN CATEGORY B AND MOST BUILDINGS IN CATEGORIES C, D AND E ARE PRIVATELY OWNED.

MENTION IN THIS BOOK DOES **NOT** ENSURE PUBLIC ACCESS.

INDEX TO MONASTIC HOUSES

ALDEBY	61, 125, 139
BEESTON REGIS	20, 50, 53, 56, 69, 73, 91, 101, 139
BINHAM	8, 50, 53, 56, 58, 59, 65, 66, 72, 81, 95, 135, 139
BLACKBOROUGH	29, 32, 87, 97, 103, 117, 119, 139
BLAKENEY	41, 47, 58, 61, 72, 139
BROMEHILL	91, 97, 99, 101, 121, 127, 139
BROMHOLME	14, 65, 81, 94, 101, 105 - 110, 116, 119, 135, 139
BUCKENHAM	71, 94, 117, 118, 139
BURNHAM NORTON	41, 47, 52, 71 - 73, 83, 139
CARBROOKE	25, 69, 101, 130, 139
CARROW	9, 27, 31, 32, 34, 57, 68, 72, 83, 89, 90, 96, 102, 112, 119, 121, 129, 132, 139
CASTLE ACRE	13, 14, 29, 50, 53, 58, 65 - 69, 71, 79, 87, 94, 99, 100, 108, 126, 128, 129, 140,
CHOSELEY	26, 140
COXFORD	83, 91, 99, 140
CRABHOUSE	17, 28 - 29, 32, 34, 36, 89, 117, 129, 140
CREAKE	19 - 20, 53, 57, 67, 83, 92, 94, 120, 123, 125, 140
DEREHAM, EAST	5, 6, 36, 140
DEREHAM, WEST	6, 22, 29, 32, 97, 101, 126, 140
DOCKING	127, 140
FIELD DALLING	16, 127, 140
FLITCHAM	97, 140
GORLESTON	42, 66, 70, 81, 82, 109, 112, 140
GUTHLAC'S STOW	125, 140
HADDISCOE	24, 141
HEACHAM	14, 141
HEMPTON	20, 86, 97, 100, 101, 141
HICKLING	45, 89, 135, 141
HORSHAM ST FAITH	9, 10, 45, 67, 72, 85, 99, 102, 111, 126, 141
HORSTEAD	16, 127, 141
INGHAM	26, 56, 58, 62, 102, 112, 114 - 116, 119, 129, 135, 141
LANGLEY	22, 73, 91, 103, 120, 141
LESSINGHAM	127, 141
LYNG	28, 101, 135, 141
LYNN PRIORY (Benedictine)	61, 65, 125, 141
LYNN AUSTIN FRIARS	42, 47, 66, 82, 110, 118, 141
LYNN BLACK FRIARS	40, 141
LYNN FRIARS OF THE SACK	48, 49, 141
LYNN GREY FRIARS	40, 62, 142
LYNN WHITE FRIARS	41, 46, 142
MARHAM	16, 30, 32, 53, 81, 83, 117, 129, 142
MASSINGHAM	20, 122, 125, 142
MODNEY	125, 127, 142

Index to monastic houses 147

MOLYCOURT	7, 98, 108, 125, 142
MOUNTJOY	76, 83, 87, 89, 98, 117, 127, 142
NORMANSBURGH	14, 142
NORWICH FRIARS OF OUR LADY	49, 142
NORWICH PIED FRIARS	49, 114, 142
NORWICH AUSTIN FRIARS	42, 46 - 48, 72, 77, 82, 142
NORWICH BLACK FRIARS	35, 36, 40, 42, 43, 45, 48 - 49, 50, 52, 54, 61 - 65, 67, 76, 90, 110, 114, 129, 130, 142
NORWICH GREY FRIARS	40, 45, 48, 79, 85, 89, 114, 142
NORWICH FRIARS OF THE SACK	45, 48, 114, 143
NORWICH WHITE FRIARS	41, 110, 114, 115, 123, 132, 143
NORWICH ST LEONARD'S	89, 125, 143
NORWICH CATHEDRAL PRIORY (HOLY TRINITY)	9, 10, 12, 53 - 54, 56, 58, 62, 68, 69, 72, 78, 81, 84, 86, 89, 90, 91, 95, 97 - 99, 101, 103, 106, 111, 118, 121, 122, 127, 128, 130, 143
PENTNEY	71, 87, 89, 143
PETERSTONE	20, 72, 125, 143
PRIOR'S THORNS	16, 95, 143
SHERINGHAM	125, 143
SHOULDHAM	22, 29, 32, 92, 104, 117, 127, 129, 130, 143
SLEVESHOLM	14, 103, 127, 143
SPORLE	127, 143
ST. BENET'S	6, 36, 45, 52 - 54, 69, 71, 72, 79, 84, 86, 87, 92, 97, 100, 101, 103, 104, 107, 109, 111, 117, 123, 125, 128, 130, 131, 143
ST. WINWALOY'S	86, 126, 143
THETFORD ST GEORGE	7, 27 - 28, 57, 127, 144
THETFORD ST MARY	14, 52, 58, 65, 66, 68, 71, 72, 80, 91, 95, 99, 100, 101, 107 - 109, 117 - 119, 120, 122, 128, 132, 144
THETFORD ST SEPULCHRE	21, 62, 89, 117, 123, 144
THETFORD AUSTIN FRIARS	46, 47, 123, 144
THETFORD BLACK FRIARS	40, 63, 85, 144
TOFT MONKS	99, 127, 144
WALSINGHAM PRIORY	18 - 19, 35, 52, 67, 88, 89, 92, 103 - 105, 108, 119, 127 - 131, 135, 144
WALSINGHAM GREY FRIARS	41, 63, 73, 144
WELL HALL	126, 144
WENDLING	51, 97, 103, 104, 106, 108, 109, 127, 144
WESTACRE	17 - 18, 67, 89, 94, 97, 101, 128, 129, 131, 144
WEYBOURNE	20, 58, 59, 62, 129, 131, 144
WEYBRIDGE	91, 127, 144
WITCHINGHAM	126, 144
WORMEGAY	89, 103, 122, 125, 145
WYMONDHAM	9, 53, 56, 58, 59, 65, 81, 84, 87, 101, 103, 110, 119, 128, 129, 155
YARMOUTH BLACK FRIARS	40, 81, 84, 90, 112, 125, 128, 145
YARMOUTH GREY FRIARS	40, 48, 54, 70, 85, 104, 111, 112, 113, 145
YARMOUTH PRIORY (Benedictine)	52, 61, 68, 86, 90, 93, 123, 125, 145
YARMOUTH WHITE FRIARS	41, 45, 46, 83, 125, 145